About the Author

Helena Morrissey is Chair-designate at AJ Bell, a FTSE 250 company whose purpose is to help people invest. She is also the Lead Non-Executive Director at the Foreign, Commonwealth and Development Office and a member of the House of Lords. Previously, Helena was CEO of Newton Investment Management for 15 years. In 2010, she founded the 30% Club to campaign for better gender-balanced company boards: today there are no all-male boards in the UK's top 350 companies, the representation of female directors has increased from less than 10 per cent to 34 per cent and there are eighteen 30% Clubs throughout the world.

Helena is the mother of nine: six girls and three boys, aged between twelve and twenty-nine.

HELENA MORRISSEY

Style and and

Substance

A guide for women who want to *win* at work

PIATKUS

PIATKUS

First published in Great Britain in 2021 by Piatkus

1 3 5 7 9 10 8 6 4 2

Copyright © 2021 Helena Morrissey
Drawings © 2021 Clara Morrissey

The moral right of the author has been asserted.

A CIP catalogue record for this book
is available from the British Library.

ISBN 978-0-349-42941-0

Typeset in Sabon by M Rules
Printed and bound in Great Britain by
Clays Ltd, Elcograf S.p.A

Papers used by Piatkus are from well-managed forests
and other responsible sources.

Piatkus
An imprint of
Little, Brown Book Group
Carmelite House
50 Victoria Embankment
London EC4Y 0DZ

An Hachette UK Company
www.hachette.co.uk

www.littlebrown.co.uk

*To my daughters Florence, Millie,
Clara, Oki, Cecily and Bea, and the next
generation of wonderful women*

Contents

Introduction

After three decades in the male-dominated finance industry, including 15 years as a CEO – alongside having nine children – I am often invited to give talks to women in business or about to start their careers. One was at Oxford University. Two of my sons were there at the time, so they came along to listen: they were the only men in the room. Afterwards they expressed surprise. Bright, ambitious, seemingly confident young women, including some of their friends, had asked questions that suggested they felt nervous about their future. They asked how to succeed in a man's world, how to combine a career with a family, how to strike the balance between fitting in and being authentic, and whether it was even possible to achieve a work–life balance in a senior role. Their tone was more anxious than excited. As my sons noted, their male friends weren't worrying about these things. They were just focused on getting a good job and counting on success after that. My sons were also surprised that their female friends hadn't raised these issues before; they only seemed comfortable discussing them in a room of (almost) all women.

Yet the questions I was asked that evening were *exactly* the same ones that come up at every such event. Although women are offered plenty of career advice, when it comes to the subjects that really concern us something seems to be lacking. Those concerns are quite rational while women at the top remain the exception, and they've been reinforced by the struggles that women have faced through the pandemic. Much of the advice we're given is badly out of date, teaching us how to fit in with past ways of working rather than how to succeed in a digital world. What's more, it tends to be defensive, focused on overcoming obstacles rather than drawing upon our strengths. We're told that three-quarters of us suffer from 'imposter syndrome' – feeling like a fraud when we are promoted to elevated positions. But while a lack of self-belief is supposedly a problem for many of us, it's apparently not great to be 'too' confident either: assertive women are said to be less likeable, and less likely to be promoted or hired. It seems we can't win. At the very least, the message is complicated: to succeed in the workplace we must learn to be both sure of ourselves and self-effacing. It feels like walking a tightrope; no wonder so many young women are more worried about making mistakes than buoyed up about their careers.

Style and Substance fills the gaps, updates the advice and starts from a very different perspective: how to best use and develop what you already have so you achieve the career success you merit. It's a practical handbook based on my real-life experiences, both as a woman in the workplace and as a business leader. It reveals what really matters when it comes to career progression today, whatever your age, situation and aspirations. It shows you how to build your own style in how you present yourself – your personal brand – and how to have confidence in that style without worrying about what might go wrong. You'll learn how to use everything you have to offer to achieve success in your own way, rather than feeling daunted about 'rules' developed by men for men in a different era. Many women feel it's all a minefield – but once you realise how much agency you have and the steps that you can take to *look* the part, *sound* the part, *feel* the part and therefore *be* the part, you'll feel empowered rather than encumbered.

We cover a lot of ground in *Style and Substance* – and that's necessary. Successful careers don't just happen off to the side of a chaotic life. You need to manage your physical and mental health, your time, your relationships at home and at work and learn how to build your confidence, even if it doesn't come naturally. We all suffer setbacks and moments of insecurity, but if you're frequently in poor health, feel very stressed, generally lack confidence or are even just dishevelled and disorganised, it's hard to make sustained progress in your career. Perfection – or anything approaching it – is *not* required. Nor do you have to be a certain personality type. This book covers each of the building blocks that together give you the best chance of success, and it explains how you can tailor them to suit your own aspirations, aptitudes and personality.

You might be surprised by the emphasis on style. I've learned that *perceptions* can make all the difference between a good or a great career. Too often, talented, capable women are overlooked because they're simply not perceived as such. The good news is that you can influence those perceptions so that you're seen to be as proficient and valuable as you truly are. It doesn't matter if you're not interested in fashion, you can still master your style at work to enhance your career. You'll also learn how to manage your time and set the agenda so that your performance is measured on results, not hours spent at the same desk, so that you can achieve the work–life balance you seek *and* be paid what you are worth. We'll consider women's health issues and normal life events such as having a baby, which really should not be workplace taboos in the 21st century. And as your own career takes off and your confidence grows, we'll look at how you can – and why you should – help other women coming along behind you.

I found as I was writing that it felt a little strange to be leaping from 'how much make-up to wear to work' to 'how to make it through artificial intelligence-based video interviews', but that's the reality of our lives. We juggle everything, generally with more success than we give ourselves credit for. I know many magnificent women who are achieving so much, whatever their area of work and despite many personal challenges. Yet now we face a new, collective threat. We've been through a tough time during the coronavirus pandemic. Lockdowns exposed the (still) huge imbalance between what men and women do at home. Progress towards gender equality has started to reverse. But we also have an opportunity to resume our onward march as more flexible working practices become the norm. Women are (at least) half the population. We must be front and centre of the recovery, not an afterthought.

I've learned through my career and life that those times when everything appears to be in a state of flux might be disconcerting but can also herald new opportunities. They are inflexion points. Now is the time for us to embrace new ways of working and show what can be achieved in our own style, secure in who we are and what we have to offer.

I hope that *Style and Substance* will give you the confidence and the resolve to do just that.

Chapter 1

What it Takes to Succeed: What They Don't Tell You but You Really Need to Know

'Leadership roles are given to those who look and act the part.'

Sylvia Ann Hewlett, founder of the Center for Talent Innovation, New York

Think of three women you admire, who inspire you. What's the first thing that comes into your mind as you consider them? I am confident that it's a mental image, a *visual* picture of each person. Perhaps you also hear their voices ringing in your ears. I thought of Mellody Hobson, chairwoman of Starbucks Corporation – the only black woman chairing one of America's top 500 public companies. Mellody is petite and graceful; her hair is styled in a flattering pixie cut. She wears glamorous clothes, often with customised embellishments, and speaks very persuasively. Next, I thought of the acclaimed fashion designer Roksanda Ilinčić, pale-skinned with long dark hair, very tall and always beautifully dressed in her own architectural designs with a trademark flash of crimson lipstick. She has a mesmerising Serbian accent and speaks softly, drawing in her listeners. Liz Truss, British Secretary of State for International Trade *and* Minister for Women and Equalities, also popped into my head, wearing one of her trademark bright fitted jackets (it happened to be blue). I've met Liz many times; she is determined to achieve results and is assured in her own views – qualities that come through in her clear voice and assertive style.

Of course, I didn't choose these women *because* of their appearances or their distinctive styles of communication – I admire them for what they have achieved. But their strong, highly individual looks, presence and poise are intertwined with their identities and successes.

First impressions count

Although we're counselled not to 'judge a book by its cover', it turns out that's exactly what we're programmed to do. Human beings respond to and process visual data better than any other type of data. The saying 'A picture is worth a thousand words' turns out to be not so far from the truth: analysis suggests that we process images up to 600 times faster than language.[1] There are numerous studies looking at how quickly we form an initial impression of someone before they say even a single word. They all conclude it's *very* quick. Princeton psychologists found that it takes us just a tenth of a second to form an opinion of a stranger from their face alone[2] – and this impression isn't significantly altered by longer exposures. That's not because we're shallow – it's one of very many mental shortcuts we make out of necessity each day to be able to get on with our lives.[3] We simply don't have time to explore every aspect of every new situation or new person, so we have learned to make snap judgements, including assessing a person's trustworthiness, capability and likeability on the basis of very little evidence.

Although these rapid-fire assessments may well be inaccurate, they tend to stick. A Cornell University study set out to examine the old adage 'you never get a second chance to make a first impression'.[4] It showed that if people form their initial judgements about someone *based on a single photo*, any negative feelings (they look unfriendly, for example) will persist six months later – even if they have actually met the person during those six months. In other words, even after having 'read a book', we *still* judge it 'by its cover'.

How perceptions hold women back

Careers are built over decades, but ultimately, it's our 'substance' – what we actually achieve – that is going to count. Many people achieve good results and work hard; some always seem to get the job, are promoted, given more responsibility, recognition and higher pay, whereas others tend to miss out – including a disproportionate number of women. The divergence between men and women's careers starts early; McKinsey & Co found in their study 'Women in the Workplace' that in 2019 women lost ground across a wide range of American companies at the very first step up to manager, *for the sixth year in a row.*[5] They analysed promotion rates at over 300 firms: for every 100 men promoted to manager, only 85 women were promoted – and this gap widened for black women (just 58 promotions) and Latinas (71). These different promotion rates meant that at the start of 2020, women held just 38 per cent of entry-level management positions. McKinsey call this the 'broken rung': it stops many women from climbing the career ladder at all. It should really come as no surprise that there are just 41 female CEOs in the Fortune 500 list of top American companies (although that's a record high) and 17 female CEOs in the UK's top 350 listed firms (also a record). There was great excitement in early 2021 when *two* African-American female CEOs made the Fortune 500 list at the same time. Up until then, there had only *ever* been two black female CEOs out of 1,800 chiefs since the list first started in 1955 – and one of those was interim, holding the post for just six months before a white man took over. There has *never* been a black female CEO of a FTSE 350 company.

What's going on? Young women are emerging from school and university better qualified than their male peers. Business leaders say that they are committed to gender equality. And over the past decade, we've seen countless special initiatives and programmes aimed at encouraging more women to succeed at work. We can't even blame COVID-19; this data was gathered before the pandemic. Neither is it because women are choosing to prioritise their families – the first rung comes before most women have children. The answer is quite simple but often overlooked: the promotion gap is linked to *perceptions* of our capabilities, and those perceptions are usually based on a masculine image of a leader. As historian Mary Beard put it so succinctly in her 'Women in Power' lecture,[6] 'Our mental, cultural template for a powerful person remains male.' Professor Beard continued, 'You cannot easily fit women into a structure that is already coded as male; you have to change the structure. That means thinking about power differently.' Being pale imitations of men won't get us very far; we need to go for the bigger prize, to 'work' what we have, as women, so that we are noticed and promoted in our own right.

I know that sounds difficult. How can we change a structure

that's stacked up against us? We need those in powerful positions today – still mainly men – to champion change, and now many are doing just that. I'm involved in multiple conversations with other business leaders – both men and women – about gender equality. Ten years ago, those conversations were focused on the numbers of female directors. Their rise gave the appearance of progress, but for the majority of women, much remained the same. Today, business leaders recognise that women bring specific strengths to the workplace and that decision-making improves when there are more of us involved at every level. Those leaders now want to create structures and cultures where far more women fulfil their career potential *as women*, not fake men.

At the same time, women need to be smart about how we navigate through a system where we *will* still encounter less enlightened attitudes.

As a graduate trainee, I missed out on the 'first rung', and when I asked what improvements I needed to make to get the promotion next time, I was told, 'Oh your performance is fine, but there's some doubt over your commitment with a baby.' My work ethic hadn't changed, my output was as high, but with my son attending a daily nursery, I was inevitably working different hours. As I reflected on any clues that might have signalled the problem, I remembered bumping into the CEO and that he'd asked about the baby rather than my investment views. At the time, I'd felt grateful for his interest in my personal life, but now I saw – belatedly – that his perceptions about me had changed. The management team now saw me as a mother rather than as a hard worker with a promising career, while I saw myself as both. With hindsight, I should have told him that my baby was thriving and then offered a few thoughts about the markets. I didn't need to hide my motherhood, but I did need to remind him that I was also still a valuable member of the investment team.

That was a long time ago and attitudes have certainly pro-gressed, but not to the point where we can assume that we will be treated fairly. As a business leader myself, I've since been involved in countless promotion discussions at which able, committed women have been described as 'needing develop-ment', even when their achievements and experience clearly stack up. I recommended a woman in my own team for promo-tion. She had glowing reviews from every single boss she had worked with at the company over many years. Any mention of her name would prompt a reaction like, 'Oh, she's just so great', and I would be asked to 'loan' her to other teams that needed her problem-solving skills and strong work ethic. But several of the *same individuals* who often praised her pushed back on my recommendation, arguing, 'She's not quite leadership material.' Their specific grounds of objection? Her tendency to play a quietly supportive role, and with that a perceived lack of presence. They never mentioned it, but she usually wore rather nondescript black from head to toe, which didn't help her create a strong visual impact. I didn't take no for an answer and she was awarded the well-deserved promotion, but I shouldn't have had to fight her corner. When it was time to tell her the good news, I (sensitively) also mentioned the issues that had been raised, along with my own observations about her style of dress, because I couldn't bear to think that she might be short-changed in future. Happily, she responded well to the feedback, and together we worked out a plan to help her better convey her capabilities. She didn't need to change who she was, but she needed to change how others saw her.

Executive presence: being seen as a leader

Results obviously matter. But the difference between a 'good' and a 'great' career is typically less to do with results, and more about others' impressions of us. 'It ain't what you do, it's the way that you do it,' sang Ella Fitzgerald (and, much later, Bananarama with the Fun Boy Three).[7] Do our colleagues and managers *think* we are authoritative? That we have strong persuasive skills? A confident body language? A compelling style of communication? That we 'look the part'? The combination of these traits is often called 'executive presence' although that's an off-putting expression. Even the word 'executive' seems out of step with what motivates us today. It might sound vaguely important, but also exclusive and remote. But as things stand, while we work towards better definitions of 'what it takes' to be a leader, women's (generally) perceived lack of executive presence is one of the main reasons why we are not promoted as often as men.

If you think I'm exaggerating about the importance of being *seen* as leadership material, take a look at the statistics for the height of male CEOs of Fortune 500 companies. Over 93 per cent of these CEOs are men. Author Malcolm Gladwell polled top American firms, asking various questions about their CEOs including their height. As he revealed in his book *Blink*, 'In the US population, about 14.5% of all men are six feet [1.83m] or over. Among [male] CEOs of Fortune 500 companies, that number is 58%.' Even more strikingly, in the general population just 3.9 per cent of adult men are six feet two inches (1.88m) or taller compared with 30 per cent of Fortune 500 male CEOs. Fewer than 3 per cent of these men are less than five feet seven. Interestingly, shorter men are over-represented among tech billionaires: Facebook's Mark Zuckerberg, Amazon's Jeff Bezos and

Bloomberg's Michael Bloomberg are all five feet seven (1.7m). It's as if they decided to turn the saying on its head: if you can't join them, beat them! If this was in any way a conscious strategy, it certainly paid off. For established companies, there is a clear bias towards promoting taller men. The explanation seems almost cartoonish: people associate an imposing physical stature with leadership qualities. My personal experience confirms this. When I've met someone for the first time, they've often blurted out, 'You're not what I expected.' They carry a mental image of what a City CEO is 'supposed' to look and sound like, and I simply don't fit that image. They knew they were meeting a woman, but the female version of the stereotypical male CEO tends to be just that, a similarly dominant and assertive variation, rather than a distinct feminine brand of power.

If we're not six-feet-tall (1.83m) men, what can we do to influence others' perceptions so that they match our capabilities? Happily, there are *many* things that we can control to improve our chances of success. (By the way, it turns out that weight has more of a bearing than height on women's careers, a subject we'll return to later.) What's more, it's very empowering when we start to understand how we can succeed. Although it upset me at the time, I eventually saw the benefits of that early career setback. It taught me to take ownership of my career, rather than simply trusting that good work and long hours would be recognised. And taking ownership included becoming aware that *every day I manifested a personal brand*, whether I liked it or not. Each of us can proactively shape our brand, rather than passively leaving it to the eye of the beholder.

It can be hard to know where to begin. My own starting point was the realisation that I needed to be more authentic. I had been dressing and acting in order to blend in, but since I was the only woman in a team of 16, this was somewhat pointless.

I vividly remember my first job interview, the grand location (a historic Cambridge college), the formidable interviewers with impressive job titles and what I wore: a dull, navy blue skirt suit, with a crisp white shirt and simple black heels. An outfit that would fit in rather than reflect my personality. I matched my attire by answering questions conservatively, anxious not to put a low-heeled foot wrong. Five years later I had failed to get the first promotion. Trying to fit in hadn't got me very far, nor had working the longest hours on the team, so why not take a different tack? I found a company where the mantra was 'no one has a monopoly on great ideas', a company that actively *sought* to employ people with different ideas and experiences. I started to dress in more feminine clothes, still professional but with more personality and 'more me'. I experimented with my hair and took presentation skills training. I gave myself a 'career makeover', and changing my appearance and learning how to communicate effectively was a big part of the transformation. To walk the fine line between being myself and being accepted, I became 'bilingual' with male colleagues – able to speak and (mostly) understand their language, office politics, the etiquette around meetings, but remaining true to my own views and style rather than adopting theirs. Seven years later, I was appointed CEO.

My story seems almost unbelievable. After falling at the first hurdle, I became a leader by acting – and dressing – like one. Yes, I worked hard and achieved results, but I'd done that in both situations.

An authoritative appearance reaps rewards

Over many years of working in a very male-dominated industry, I learned that working out what gave me an *air* of authority helped me to actually gain that authority. *And to do that, I didn't need to act – or dress – like a man.* When I cast off the pinstriped trouser suit (yes, I really did wear one in the 1990s) in favour of more feminine clothes and behaved as though I meant business *on my terms*, others assumed I did and gave me more opportunities to contribute and perform. As you read on, you'll see a pattern among women who are now in their forties or older: we have all gone through a trouser suit phase before realising that mimicking men wasn't bringing out the best in us.

It's exciting to see young female politicians such as Alexandria Ocasio-Cortez, who is the youngest woman ever to serve in the US Congress and is very much doing things her way. 'AOC' is vocal. She's also a consummate power dresser, favouring sharp suiting and midi-dresses combined with signature red lipstick, slicked-back middle-parted hair and gold hoop earrings. Like my former colleague who so deserved her promotion, AOC wears a lot of black – but her structured and honed outfits are anything *but* nondescript, and she varies her look with occasional brights. In the UK, Kemi Badenoch, Member of Parliament and Minister for Equalities, Children and Families (and the mother of three), gave her lively maiden speech (she quoted Woody Allen on sex – 'if it's not messy, you're not doing it right' – drawing a parallel with democracy) wearing a fabulous cobalt-blue dress and with her hair in her hallmark long braids. Kemi is always photo-graphed in sleek dresses and suits, usually in strong colours; she looks put-together, businesslike – and authentic. Neither of these impressive young politicians (with very different political views) has adopted the male trappings of power, nor have they tried to submerge their differences. They are their own women.

There is no diktat around how to dress for success – and that's the point. It's about discovering what works for you, what makes you feel the best version of yourself. I have some very stylish, successful female friends. Each has their own 'style signifiers'. Anya Hindmarch, the handbag and accessories supremo, often wears sweeping, voluminous coats, usually in a dark colour. Her long blonde hair looks wonderful against black. Anya also wears bold necklaces, big black spectacles and – as you'd expect – carries quirky bags of her own design. She pulls off all this drama magnificently. Sian Westerman – banker and member of the British Fashion Council board – surprises in clothes that are experimental with volume, shape and unusual details. Sian is petite, and while some women of her height would shy away from such bold designs, Sian shows who's boss by the way she carries them off. My great friend Baroness Mary Goudie is a global advocate for the rights of women and children – we first met through her work on combating human trafficking. Mary, who's now in her seventies, is very elegant and wears polished shift dresses with matching coats and gorgeous Italian bags by lesser-known brand Gianfranco Lotti.

Each of these accomplished women has great confidence in their own looks. I've known them all for many years. They've tended to play up those looks more surely with age, and I'm inspired whenever we meet. People have confidence in confident people. Fortunately (and as you'll see), there are techniques that can help you to exude more confidence than you might actually feel. (Note: when I refer to confidence, I'm not talking about domineering behaviour or brash overconfidence – I'm referring to the inner strength that comes from having faith in yourself.) My turning point came when I stopped trying to disappear into the background, stopped thinking in terms of 'this might be wrong' and instead consciously approached my image from the perspective that 'this might be right'. And, as I was experimenting, there were a few moments when I realised what worked. A top salesman who was new to the firm approached me after our morning meeting (a common practice in investment teams, where analysts and fund managers share news and views): would I do a roadshow to promote my funds? At the time, he really couldn't have known whether the funds I was managing were any good. He told me that he'd been impressed by my performance at the meeting. Quite frankly, I knew I hadn't said anything of particular note, but I had spoken confidently and was wearing a favourite cream skirt suit, plain but sharply cut, with heels that gave me extra height: a strong, feminine look and one that made me *feel* authoritative. In that moment, I really understood the meaning of 'power dressing'. Instead of blending in, I was putting across my technical knowledge in a style that – finally – gave me an edge.

Be in control of your personal brand

Style is, after all, so much more than just clothes. It's a reflection of attitude and how we share our personal story, our 'inner life' with the world. The iconic Kate Moss lives by the mantra, 'Never complain, never explain' and has rarely given interviews. Instead, she has let her inimitable style – and her colourful life – do the talking. I remember admiring a look she was photographed wearing with trademark insouciance: skinny black jeans, flat ballet pumps pulled together with a fabulous silk trench coat. Kate Moss was expressing her strong personality through what was superficially a simple, even classic, outfit *by the way that she wore it*: casually, defiantly, powerfully. She had created and was in control of her distinctive personal brand.

Fortunately, we don't need to reach anything like Kate Moss's mastery of style for our image to help our careers. I've had many opportunities to observe lots of wonderful, successful and diverse women, and I can see that developing a winning style has nothing to do with being a certain age, height or body shape, obeying specific rules, following trends, spending a fortune or being beautiful. Some of my friends and colleagues are at the very top of their chosen careers, others are young women starting out, returning to work after a baby or making their next big career move. *Everyone* suffers from moments of insecurity, but the women I'm thinking of are generally comfortable in their own skin. They are all shapes and sizes, every colour and creed, young and not so young; they work in corporate, charitable, public and creative sectors and some love fashion, whereas others feel indifferent about it. But they understand what works for them and they are empowered by the knowledge that style and presence count. They don't spend endless time in front of the mirror or in the shops, or splurge all the money they've worked so hard to earn on outfits for work. They've developed a look and a style of communicating that suits their personality and situation. You can do the same. In turn, you will gain control of how you are perceived. You will be setting the agenda, not limited by prejudice or what's gone before. And if there's no exact role model? Well if no one's got there already, why not be the first to achieve what you want, in the style you want to achieve it?

Although I'm confident that your efforts will be rewarded, the impact on your career might not be immediate or dramatic. Looking (or sounding) the part might contribute only a small initial advantage when we are seeking a job, a promotion, a pay rise, or a new opportunity. But the cumulative effect after several decades is significant. Women clearly have the merit to progress, but, as we've already established, if we're not *seen* as being up to the job we won't be given it. The solution is to stack the odds more in our favour at each and every stage, by ensuring that we use *all* the tools at our disposal: our knowledge, experience, networks, aptitude *and* attitude, self-assured body language and a clear voice and style. To be able to do all that, we need to take care of the precursors to feeling confident and 'put-together': our health, our time and the milestones in our life, such as pregnancy and maternity leave. Since the pandemic, we must add a new skill: the ability to perform online. This sounds like a lot to cope with, but we can break it down into manageable steps. The more holistic approach and effort is certainly worth it. By capitalising on everything we have to offer rather than a small subset of our abilities, we are far more likely to succeed. And as we do, we'll be able to change that masculine stereotype of a leader, helping the next generation of women.

At present, however, the standard development training we're given at work or for a job interview has many critical gaps. We might be given some advice about body language and how to project our voice for presentations, but many of the factors that can help us exude confidence and authority – including clothes, hair and make-up – are completely omitted. They're seen as frivolous or embarrassing, even if everyone knows that they really can make a difference. The exclusions place women at a disadvantage in a world of work established by men. Corporate dress codes don't help much, they tend to be either too vague ('dress for your day') or too prescriptive. (In 2010, Swiss bank UBS produced a 44-page corporate dress guide covering everything from the colour and size of suits to the length of toenails. It even dictated flesh-coloured underwear, provoking much merriment.) This book fills the advice gap so that you can find – or fine-tune – your individual career-enhancing style.

And yet ... I have to admit that it's taken me many years to truly find my own. Along the way, I've made bad wardrobe choices, and there have been times where I've had very little money to spend on clothes, a distorted body image, lots of shape-shifting challenges (nine successful pregnancies and two miscarriages, breastfeeding, plus several vein and foot operations requiring clothes to hide very unglamorous surgical stockings) and unfortunate haircuts and colours, including a long phase of almost black hair that drained all the colour from my face. (There are horrible photos to remind me.) There have been times when I really haven't bothered much about my appearance, usually coinciding with feeling generally exhausted. My career-dressing experiences have been a mix of successes and failures, just like my actual career. But the mistakes have helped me to understand what works, including for lockdown when dressing for my day meant considering how to literally run from Zoom calls to walk the dog, check on my school-age children doing their online lessons, load the washing machine and drier – then back again to my desk to join yet another call (before repeating the routine).

The pandemic has created a raft of extra pressures for women. As well as bearing the brunt of extra domestic chores, home-schooling and elder care, women are over-represented in those sectors hit hardest by the economic downturn – hospitality, leisure, beauty and retail shops – and face a greater risk of unemployment. During lockdown, many of us had little time to think about anything other than the essential tasks in our day ahead. We now find ourselves at a crossroads for gender equality and perhaps for our own careers. One path takes us back to more traditional roles and fewer career opportunities while the other offers a tantalising glimpse of more flexible ways of working in the future and better-balanced lives. If we're going to recover and move forward from this crisis, we need to invest precious time and energy in ourselves.

Before turning to how you can create your own winning approach, let's recap what you need to bear in mind.

Takeaways from Chapter 1

1. A key to career progression lies in perceptions. This isn't about changing who you are; it's about managing how people perceive you.

2. You are more likely to be promoted to leadership roles if you 'look and act the part'. People *do* judge a book by its cover. You might be tempted to emulate men, since the stereotype of a leader is masculine, but the most exciting young women today are fashioning both their appearance and their careers on their own terms. Authenticity is increasingly prized. If your style reflects what you have to offer, you'll find it easier to build your confidence and to succeed.

3. You don't need to be an expert or even interested in fashion. You can enhance your career by taking simple steps to build a strong personal brand. It just requires some time and thought.

4. There are many facets to developing that personal brand. We will consider your style of appearance and communication and the need to take care of yourself and to manage your time, as well as ensuring that life events don't derail your career. A holistic approach is more likely to yield success than narrowly focusing on a subset of 'what it takes'.

Chapter 2

Defining Your Personal Brand and Finding Your Style: the Personality, Values, Experience and Expertise You Want the World to See

'Style is something each of us already has, all we need to do is find it.'

Diane von Furstenberg,
fashion designer and style icon

Let's start with style of dress, since it's often overlooked when it comes to career advice, yet it can be so valuable in helping us to create a good impression.

Some lucky people are naturally stylish. They know what suits them and always look good and entirely appropriate, whatever the occasion. They wear their clothes, rather than letting their clothes wear them, and everything about them creates a strong personal brand. DJ, broadcaster, musician, author and mother of two, Lauren Laverne is a good example. In early 2020, Lauren interviewed me as a 'castaway' on *Desert Island Discs*.[8] When we posed for photographs afterwards I was struck by her self-possession. With a lilting north-east accent, Lauren's speaking voice is great for radio, but she also had no need to glance in the mirror, touch up her make-up or straighten her clothes. She knew exactly how to look into the camera, composed and controlled. Images of Lauren taken over the years (she's now in her early forties) show a remarkably consistent approach, creating a down-to-earth yet glamorous image. Feminine (lots of floral prints, colours, flirty dresses) *and* 'cool' (choppy blonde hair, nothing prim or contrived), Lauren's style suits her looks and reflects how she wants to be seen – and by whom. She makes it look effortless, but it turns out that Lauren thinks carefully about what she wears, saying, 'It's part of my identity, I've always liked dressing in something that makes me feel better, I can . . . just do a better job.'[9]

Closer to (my) home, my eldest daughter Florence has always known what suits her. Even as a small child she veered towards the bohemian – I have kept a purple shearling Afghan coat with an 'age 8' label that looks straight from the 1970s, although Flo was eight in 2002. As she grew up, her style evolved into a more modern, streamlined version of the look: both artistic and chic. I will see an unusual dress and think: *that's so Flo*. Her idiosyncratic style is also a reflection of who she is. Flo has forged her own path rather than copying her peers or siblings. They've all gone to university, but Flo was adamant that that wasn't for her. A singer-songwriter, she left school at 17 with a recording contract. She marches beautifully to her own tune and her clothes echo that.

Such clarity doesn't come easily to most of us, but we can each develop a style that reflects who we are and enhances our chances of success at work and in life. Our style is how we present ourselves to the world, our personal brand is how others see us, and the two are inextricably linked. But the truth is that most of us don't spend much time thinking about our 'brand'. For a start, it might seem narcissistic. We live in a look-at-me world and that can feel unhealthy and unappealing. But we're not talking here about being self-obsessed or overly fixated on appearances. Remember that others make inferences about you based on what they see and hear. It's not vain to give this some thought – it's smart.

We're also often very busy, immersed in multiple tasks. Our days end up being strung together, occurrences small and large joining up to influence the direction of our lives. We have successes and setbacks along the way, and there are moments when we plan ahead or consciously take a decision over something that feels momentous, but most of the time we're hardly even aware of the multiple small decisions we make each day. We just get on with the business of living.

If you ever have the opportunity of career coaching or mentoring, your teacher will encourage you to stand back from the day-to-day and think about the direction you want to take, the goals you aspire to, what you might need to work on and who you might need to convince to help you reach them. It's hard to benefit from the coaching unless you have at least a vague idea of where you are heading. Similarly, if you're going to develop a personal brand and style that works for you, the first step is to stand back and consider (truthfully) what defines you and what you hope to achieve. This isn't a gazing-off-into-the-distance 'Who am I?' ponder along the lines of Charlie Sheen's character in *Wall Street* (subsequently spoofed in *Zoolander 2*), but a more prosaic analysis of your personality and values along with an awareness of what and who might help you to succeed.

Look at where you are now

Style starts with knowing who you are – and what you want to become. Consider the following questions:

1. What do you really care about? (Your focus)
2. What are your main personality traits? (Your starting point)
3. What are your goals? (You might need to adapt to achieve them, to dial your natural style up or down)
4. Who might you need to convince? (Your target audience)
5. What story do you want to tell in how you present yourself? (To engage your audience)

The answers will help to clarify the core elements of your personal brand and the foundations of your style. At this stage, we're just looking for *principles* to guide you. There are no right or wrong answers. Here are mine.

What do I really care about? What am I focused on? My family is the most important focus for me. I also love having a fulfilling career. I've felt fortunate in being able to combine the two, and that's the driving force behind my work on gender equality, to help more women enjoy their family life *and* have successful careers.

What are my main personality traits? According to standard psychometric tests, I'm innately introverted and altruistic. As we saw in the previous chapter, my original 'style' (if it could be described as such) was aimed at blending in, deliberately *not* drawing attention to myself. As my career took off, I became more confident about how I dressed but was still a low-profile businesswoman. But that altruistic trait means that I'm also inclined to challenge things that don't seem right and to create change – even if that might make my life difficult. Sometimes this has required more courage than I thought I could muster as I've 'put myself out there', including on social media. Even if I've been nervous doing so, I've been willing to take positions that some might find unexpected or controversial. As I've sought to help more women succeed through campaigns like the 30% Club,* this tendency to shake things up has become the defining characteristic of my personal brand.

What are my goals? Who do I need to convince to help me reach them? My goals are a happy family *and* more women fulfilling their potential. Those are two very big ambitions with two very different 'target audiences'! The first involves nurturing a small(ish) group of people I'm very close to, the second demands ideas, actions, a timetable and good relationships with the media to amplify messages. I dress in a fairly invisible, practical way at home but ramp things up for campaigning. I learned to speak in a media-friendly way (shorter sentences, clearer points) and to dress in a more eye-catching style, turning up the volume by choosing stronger colours or quirkier shapes. By practising, by taking on more public speaking and media opportunities, I've become less introverted. I have consciously and consistently remained feminine: the message I want to convey is that

---

* I founded the 30% Club in 2010 with the aim of achieving at least 30 per cent women on UK corporate boards through voluntary business-led change. At the time, less than 10 per cent of board roles on the top FTE 350 companies were held by women. The 30 per cent goal was met in 2019. There are now eighteen 30% Clubs throughout the world and the initiative is led by Ann Cairns, Vice-Chair at Mastercard.

women bring our own qualities to bear, rather than needing to be honorary men.

What story do I want to tell in how I present myself? My personal brand started as classic and ordinary and has evolved to be deliberately more impactful, perhaps even exuberant, to help meet my goals. I dress to make an impression before I speak. I want to appear confident that those goals will be reached. I've learned that a positive approach can create momentum in itself – people are inclined to join in if something *looks* successful. That's a lot to ask of an outfit, but I do try to think about the effect that a particular dress, or even choice of colour, will have at public moments. My core style is consistent but adjusted to resonate with specific audiences.

I'm in my fifties and have had a long time to develop my personal brand and style. The clarity around my 'purpose' has sharpened with age. What if you're at an earlier point in your career and perhaps less sure about yourself? I asked my 22-year-old daughter Millie who's just embarking on a career in financial services to answer the same questions and to frame her ambitions in terms of the next three to five years rather than trying to think too far ahead.

What do you really care about, Millie? My family is very important to me. I value my friendships and always try to be kind to people. I enjoy working and studying hard. Having finished my degree in Sanskrit, I'm now working at a really interesting company that invests in and advises companies based in Africa. It has a clear social purpose – I wanted even my first role to be one where I can contribute something positive, as well as taking steps to become more independent. I'm focusing on learning, doing the best work I can and building a network. I also really enjoy playing sports. I took up korfball (a cross between basketball and netball played by teams of eight: four men and four women) at university and have now joined a London club. [Millie is being modest. She played for the first team, won her half-blue and was twice part of the winning Oxford side at the Varsity match.]

What are your main personality traits? I'm very organised. I'm quite introverted and happy to work by myself on a task. I'm reliable, trustworthy and thoughtful, but I'd also describe myself as determined and ambitious. I don't always feel very confident, but I know my own mind and am a self-starter. At the same time, I'm aware that there's a huge amount I have to learn, so I read a lot and am very happy to take guidance or be mentored by someone a few years ahead of me. I'm very open to ideas at this stage in my life and I love learning.

What are your goals? Who might you need to convince to achieve them? Over the next five years, I'd like to be well under way in my career, enjoying my job and living in my own home but still seeing my family often and playing sport regularly. I'd like to be in a happy relationship and to feel confident. I'm going to need to be perceived positively at work so that my career develops.

What story do you want to tell in how you present yourself? I hope that people see me as reliable, as someone who works hard and is willing to take on a wide variety of tasks. I can be trusted to deliver. My style is neat and classic, nothing adventurous, so the two are aligned. I like fitted (but not tight) clothes, nothing droopy or baggy. I don't want to wear anything too formal and structured – that doesn't feel 'me', but I do want to look put-together. Through earlier internships I have worked out a 'uniform' that I'm happy with for work: coloured poplin fitted shirts, pencil skirts, neat suits with short skirts, fitted trousers, loafers. My look doesn't convey a very distinctive message perhaps, but it does reflect who I am right now and it seems appropriate for an office environment. I feel comfortable in these clothes.

At such an early point in her career, it's no surprise that Millie is somewhat tentatively forming her workwear style. I chair the Diversity Project, which is on a mission to attract diverse talent (including more women) and create an inclusive culture in the investment industry, one of the most traditional and male-dominated sectors. Suman Sidhu, 27, is one of the Project's leading lights. She's an investment consultant and qualified actuary, six years into her career. Suman helped to launch a podcast series, 'Spotlight on Women in Investments', encouraging up-and-coming female investment professionals to raise their profile and talk about their experiences. I've always been impressed by Suman's confidence, direct style of communication and polish: she is proactive, thoughtful and a wonderful ambassador for young women in finance.

I asked Suman the same questions.

What do you really care about, Suman? As clichéd as it might sound, I am focused on being a 'good person', which can have many definitions! I have increasingly realised the importance of self-development to ensure that I am being a great daughter, sister, friend and colleague. I have a small circle of family and friends who are very important to me. I am a minority in lots of ways in the City: I am a young brown woman with a northern accent whose parents emigrated from India; my siblings and I are the first generation to go to university. Although I've always been keen to progress both in my personal and professional life, more recently I've realised that I can really help other people who might feel like outsiders to realise their true potential, too. I believe my bigger purpose is to help others.

What are your main personality traits? I would describe myself as confident, motivated and determined. From a very young age, I was constantly asking questions. I'm still naturally curious. My parents got divorced when I was 16 and sitting my GSCEs, and although I'm not the eldest of my siblings I became the strong one for the rest of the family. I threw myself into my studies and ended up with 11 A*s. That experience made me feel that I needed to be in control of my life and independent. In the past, I have been reluctant to show much emotion, but since I started working with clients I've realised that it's important to connect with people. My colleagues say that I'm a 'mother hen' – during lockdown I realised that I was coping better than some members of the team and ended up being a mentor for those who were finding it hard. As I get older, I've become more comfortable with challenging the norm and not just speaking up, but also taking action.

What are your goals? Who might you need to convince to achieve them? My broad goals are being the best version of myself and helping others to do the same. I'd like to continue progressing in my career. The goal is to ultimately have a family and nice home alongside a successful career where I am driving change for the better. The company I've been working at for the past two years, Lane Clark & Peacock, is great about supporting my work with the Diversity Project and with women's networks. Their approach has always been to trust me to run with it when I find worthwhile causes that I want to be involved with. Over the past 18 months or so I've been very focused on building my personal brand, including using LinkedIn to highlight my work on gender equality – I want my network to think of me as someone who represents diversity (in many dimensions) in finance *and* encourages other people to achieve their goals.

What story do you want to tell in how you present yourself? My style is always changing and it very much reflects how I want to feel at a certain point. I take care over my appearance not because I feel I have to but because it helps me feel better and more confident: if I'm dressed the part, that really helps me rise to the occasion. I realised quite early on that first impressions count; I was forming rapid judgements about people when I met them, so they must be doing the same about me. At work my 'story' is all about being confident. This takes the form of a smart, classic and, above all, comfortable style. I don't follow fast-fashion trends but stick with things that I deem will always be in fashion. I love high-waisted wide-legged trousers, blazers worn with great tops. I'm not copying men's suits – these are fluid, feminine clothes, I'm just more comfortable in trousers than tight-fitting dresses and skirts. I want to show I can be myself in how I dress for work, and that it's the best version of me. Hopefully, that will encourage others to do the same.

As you can see, these are very personal and wide-ranging reflections from three people at very different career stages. Millie, Suman and I all work in finance – and perhaps surprisingly, given it's not what people might immediately associate with this profession, we are all very purpose-driven. We want accurate judgements to be made about us, based on our work, our relationships, our 'content' (including on social media) and our appearance – so we take care that our style of dress reflects who we are. Your answers are yours alone, and hopefully you'll see how your personality and values already influence your current style. But the aspirational aspect is important, too: your style today might need to evolve to help you achieve your goals. We're focusing now on finding out what makes you feel comfortable and confident, but keep an open mind – that comfort zone might need challenging as your life and career unfold.

Your style tribe

Your character is the starting point for finding a style that you're really happy with. Your personal taste is the next building block.

It's sometimes suggested that we each fall into a style tribe where 'birds of a feather flock together'. Ultimately, there are as many styles as there are women, but it might help you to feel clearer about your preferences if you consider the following words and pick out two, possibly three, that resonate most.

adventurous	edgy
androgynous	elegant
artistic	feminine
bohemian	fun
chic	gamine
classic	glamorous
colourful	maximalist
comfortable	minimalist
conservative	modern
demure	relaxed
eclectic	romantic

I'm drawn to 'modern' and 'feminine'. I've used the word 'feminine' several times already, but such clothes need to be cut in a modern way with clean lines to avoid being too girly for my age and work. No puffy sleeves, tiered skirts or frills. Anne O'Leary, CEO of Vodafone Ireland, describes her style as 'fun' and 'feminine'. She's also a fan of dresses and favours quirky designs that bring a smile to her colleagues' faces. But style is not a straitjacket: Jenny Halpern Prince, founder and CEO of communications agency Halpern, advises many influencers and suggests, 'Your personal style is a visual explanation of who you are. That doesn't mean always wearing the same things; you can be a bit of a chameleon depending on what you're doing – there may be a corporate side, a fun and relaxed side, a more glamorous or rock chick side to who you are – but there will be a thread running throughout your different looks.'

Our character comes first, our taste second – and of course the two are likely to overlap. But we also feel the need to dress *appropriately.* There are some companies where everyone dresses casually. In 2007, one of Google's recruiters offered advice on what to wear for an interview at the firm, 'Sales and operations people wear quality shirts, nice slacks or khakis, and Ecco shoes. You can get away with wearing Dockers. Everyone else wears jeans, T-shirts, and UGG boots. Leave the Rolex at home. Don't dress for the job you want to have, dress 30% above your level. More than that, and it will look like you're trying too hard.'[10] I've been to Google's London offices several times. With a little updating (swap the UGGs for trainers) and anglicising, the advice still stands (for both men and women), and it applies to other tech companies, too. Other careers require formal dress: female barristers appearing in court are expected to wear plain black or dark dresses, skirts below the knee or trousers (only permitted since 1995) with a white shirt and dark shoes (no skyscraper heels).[11] These extremes might be limiting but they are clear-cut – it's the wide spectrum in between that can feel tricky to navigate.

In fact, every firm and every sector seems to have a slightly different rule book. Very many women tell me that they find this broad topic of 'appropriateness' daunting, especially if they work in a sector that is male-dominated, where they feel the pressure to conform and yet are clearly different because of their gender. Add in the fashionable edict to be 'your authentic self' and it's no surprise that the messages seem contradictory and confusing.

There's no formula for appropriateness

Let's look at real-life examples of women getting it both right and wrong for practical clues of appropriateness.

At the first firm I worked at, there were literally only four senior women across the entire New York and London offices, although it employed several thousand people at the time. Although these women had blazed an impressive trail, they worked all hours of the day and night and tended to act tough, speak stridently and dress in a masculine way as well. One stood out: she spoke softly and dressed beautifully, with trademark silk scarves, elegant fitted jackets and skirts, with glossy understated hair and make-up. She was quite revered by the younger women in the office, including me. Her style was by no means 'pushing the envelope', but her predilection for skirts and feminine tailoring was ahead of the time, making her appear supremely confident. She was the first woman appointed as a director of the firm, and she showed that 'getting it right' at the time involved quite subtle – yet highly effective – adjustments to the masculine uniform.

By way of contrast, I once interviewed someone for a leadership role at a charity. The successful candidate needed to develop strong relationships with senior executives at the companies who supported the charity's work. We were down to the last two candidates, both well qualified on paper. One arrived in clothes that would be just fine in a corporate setting but sported pink hair and Doc Martens. It seemed a bit provocative – especially for a job interview. But she seemed a strong candidate, so my co-interviewer and I made a point of talking about the conservative supporter base and how she would need to engage with senior executives. We invited her back for another chat. The Doc Martens remained, but this time her hair was blue. If she had kept one or other of her trademarks, we could have moved forwards. Keeping *both* seemed to be goading us.

We can tie ourselves in knots over the issue of appropriateness when it's really just a question of being aware and respectful of our environment. A Mohican haircut wouldn't suit an accountancy job. A frumpy navy suit would be questionable if you're working for a fashion magazine. Avoid extremes. I deliberately left out certain 'style tribes' in the list above – punk, rebellious, outrageous, dull, dreary, drab – for that (obvious) reason. But you don't need to adhere slavishly to what's gone before, especially if your workplace is very male-dominated.

When I started my career 30 years ago, workplace culture in financial and professional services firms was stacked against women and femininity; the norm was command-and-control, hierarchical and 'macho'. It was hardly surprising that women tended to adopt the male trappings of power to succeed – often at high personal cost. I attended a talk given by an American lawyer, about 15 years older than me, who had reached the top of her field. She explained that 'on her way up' in the 1980s she had been given a year-long assignment in a remote and distant part of the country as part of a test to see if she had what it took to make partner. (This wasn't conjecture, her boss eventually told her.) It meant leaving her two-year-old son for the entire week, starting every Sunday evening. She described how he would sob uncontrollably as she left for the airport. The lawyer's own daughter was now a mother and a lawyer herself and was refusing to do anything even approaching this level of sacrifice for the sake of her career, to her mother's concern – and the audience's relief. We were horrified by the idea that a man would set a woman such a cruel test – something that he did not ask his male colleagues to do.

Those very few women who reached the pinnacle decades ago achieved their success despite all the obstacles put in their way, learning to 'play the game' even if they didn't feel particularly happy. Their sacrifices were both real and disheartening. Although it's unfinished business, workplace cultures have been shifting to be more welcoming of difference, especially over the last ten years. It's now recognised that leadership styles have become more inclusive and flexible – even in the military. Surgeon Captain Kate Prior, one of the most senior women in the Royal Navy, describes the shift over her 28-year naval career from 'top-down' leadership to 'leading from the front', power-sharing to 'capture the benefits of different perspectives'.[12] Uniformity of opinion is seen as undesirable today, and in many walks of life, we're invited to dress less uniformly as well. The prevalence of digital remote working during the pandemic has accelerated the trends: even the boss isn't working from home in a suit and tie (with a few exceptions).

This is good news for women who've been waiting a long time to be able to flourish in our own way. Whereas copying men might have been the only way for women starting out several decades ago, it's not necessarily the right approach today given the increasing recognition that we add value being ourselves. The world needs more leaders who are empathetic, collaborative and more representative of the population – in other words, *more women*. In fact, studies show that women tend to outperform men in 17 out of 19 traits considered desirable in leaders.[13] We don't need to pretend to be second-class men: we are first-class women.[14] What's more, each of us is unique, bringing our own ideas, gifts and diverse perspectives to the table.

Breaking the rules to dress authentically

We need to extend our ambition to dressing authentically. As I realised in my thirties, if we feel more able to be ourselves, we're likely to perform better. That might require breaking with convention like that inspiring woman at my first firm – and today we can push those frontiers further. The shops haven't really caught up yet. I popped into a well-known high-street fashion store recently and noticed that they had a 'career dressing' rail. All the separates were black. Boring jackets, skirts and trousers, with the odd shift dress in grey or navy and a few basic white or striped shirts: a (very slightly) adapted version of the male professional uniform. The thinking is not intentionally anti-women. Men's dark classic suits, often worn with a crisp white shirt, do project conventional authority. They are smart but not showy – seemingly trustworthy. And although men might want more choice (and are given it in many workplaces these days) it makes for an easy office dress code. But as we've established, it might be easy but not right if it obscures what's really great about us. In 2018 *Tatler* magazine ran a story, 'The New Power Dressing – How to Dress for Work Now'. The author, Serena Hood, declared:

> Finally! – women are shunning the drab grey suits people put on to instil an air of authority. In doing so, their less austere looks convey a more powerful subconscious statement to peers than ill-fitting shoulder pads ever could.

Yet, in addition to the rather depressingly dull definition of 'career dressing' on the high street, there are still many subliminal rules around our appearance and behaviour. We often pick them up by osmosis, overhearing criticism of other women. (Yes, we have ears!) Sadly, it's more a list of don'ts than dos. We learn that we shouldn't be too assertive (bossy) or too passive (not leadership material), too shrill (irritating) or too quiet (again, not leadership material). We should wear make-up (to look polished) but not too much (inappropriate) or too little (suggests we don't care). We should avoid certain hairstyles (so many pitfalls here), be neither overweight (suggests a lack of self-discipline) nor underweight (mental health issues), to take care of our bodies (stamina, energy, commitment) and to be put-together at all times even while working long hours (ditto). The list is endless and exhausting!

My advice is simple: *stop worrying about these rules*. When we're worried about breaking a rule, we tend to behave very differently than if we are looking to capitalise on a strength. If we're trying to avoid displeasing someone, we protect the downside and err on the side of caution. When we're trying to impress someone, we'll go for it! There may be times when it's right to be cautious, but if you're looking to establish a strong presence, you need to take a more positive approach. You are an intelligent person who can judge what works best for you and is appropriate in the context of your workplace. The only real noes are quite obvious: no ultra-tight or very short mini-skirts, no plunging necklines, flip-flops, sliders or shorts, and avoid any 'extreme' looks. You know who you are and you are either clear about what you want to achieve or at least you are starting to think about it. Let's call this your style DNA. Now it's time to work out what suits your specific body shape, colouring and budget. We can then put this all together to create your own winning style and strong personal brand.

Let's first remind ourselves of the precursors of finding the style that works for you.

Takeaways from Chapter 2

1. Your style should reflect your personality, circumstances and aspirations – the starting point is self-awareness. These aspects will change over time and over the course of your career – your style is likely to evolve.

2. Appropriateness can feel a daunting challenge. A common-sense approach works better than trying to adhere to endless rules. If you're unsure, take it one step at a time. If you are aware and respectful of your environment, you'll be fine.

3. Striking a balance between authenticity and fitting in is often another dilemma, especially for women working in male-dominated environments. The days of women needing to dress like a man to succeed are largely over. Today, women are increasingly valued for what we offer. It can take a bit of practice and time to build the confidence to wear what really suits us, but it's worth persevering since we perform better when we feel able to be ourselves.

Chapter 3

How to Dress for Success: the Fundamentals – Dressing for Your Life, Your Body, Your Personality and Your Budget

'Start where you are. Use what you have. Do what you can.'

Arthur Ashe (1943–1975), Grand Slam-winning tennis champion and still the only black man to win Wimbledon and the US and Australian Opens

Dressing for success might sound appealing, but even if you have a clear idea of what you'd like your personal brand to be, it can be hard to know where to start. I certainly struggled with a combination of not really knowing what *suited* me, a lack of money at various points, a lack of time since becoming a mother, and, for many years, a negative view of my appearance. Sadly, I'm far from alone. In 2019 the Mental Health Foundation found that 36 per cent of women of all ages had experienced stress over their body image to the extent of feeling 'unable to cope'.[15] In America, nine out of ten women say they are dissatisfied with their bodies.[16]

These are depressing statistics. There are many reasons for this pervasive lack of body confidence (which also applies to men, although male body image issues are less well researched); an obvious one is the prevalence of social-media images of perfection. Many Instagram images are edited to (vastly) improve reality,* but that doesn't stop us comparing ourselves unfavourably. Our self-images are also often terribly distorted, as if we were gazing at ourselves in one of those crazy funfair mirrors.

Our circumstances can trigger body image issues

I suffered from anorexia as a teenager and then again in my early twenties, just as I was starting work. In the first episode of my illness, I weighed just five stone (31.75kg) (I had nearly reached my full adult height, five feet seven inches/1.7m) and yet *I thought I was fat*. At 21 years old, I was working incredibly long hours (usually 14-hour days) in hectic New York and I ate a salad at lunch and a bagel for supper. Nothing else. That crazy mirror really was working overtime.** Unsurprisingly, even the smallest size clothes began to overwhelm my ever-shrinking frame and, although for the first time in my life (and, it turned out, rather briefly) I had money to spend on clothes, I would return from

---

* For full transparency, I only ever use 'filters' on my posts to brighten colours and improve lighting.
** Anorexia and other eating disorders are serious mental health conditions, characterised by distorted thoughts and delusions. If you believe you are at risk or suffering from an eating disorder, contact https://www.beateatingdisorders.org.uk/support-services/helplines for advice and support.

the shops empty-handed. I would traipse around the department stores, mesmerised by Bloomingdale's in particular, occasionally plucking up the courage to try something on, only to always decide that it looked hideous on me.

New York was exciting but daunting for a girl just out of university who'd grown up in small English villages. There's no doubt in my mind that my descent back into anorexia was borne out of feeling lonely and overwhelmed. When I returned to the UK two years later and was reunited with friends, family and (my now husband) Richard, I recovered. I looked better, and normal clothes fitted again, but now I had no money! I'd spent the savings amassed in those two years in New York paying off Richard's negative equity after the property market collapsed soon after he'd bought a flat with a friend. I was happy to do it – the money had seemed like a windfall, and we could then start married life with a clean financial sheet. But by the time we'd rebuilt our finances, we had young children ... and I had no time to go clothes shopping. (This was pre-online.) The lesson from this tale of woe is *not to wait* for the stars to align, or that moment when you feel good about yourself, have money and time to spare *and* the enthusiasm to experiment and develop your style, because that moment might simply never happen. Instead, build things gradually, starting from exactly where you are in life.

Today I would tell my young New York-dwelling self to avoid the upmarket department stores where all the other shoppers seemed perfect, reinforcing my insecurities. Instead, I'd urge her to visit some of the more youthful American stores (which also ran smaller sizes aimed at adolescent shoppers), such as Banana Republic and J. Crew. I'd tell her to use the opportunity of living in New York to invest in some wonderful American brands, focusing on accessories, since they didn't require her to be a certain dress size: Cole Haan for shoes, Coach for bags, Ralph Lauren for belts. Later, when she was back in London and money was tight, I'd suggest second-hand stores, especially the ones around Knightsbridge and the Kings Road, which benefit from donations from wealthy residents. And when children came along and there was no time to go shopping, to experiment and create new looks by pairing different items in her existing wardrobe rather reaching for the same outfits every day. Most of all, I'd encourage my younger self to have a little more fun with workwear dressing and to see the challenges as a game to win.

Before you can dress for success, you need to believe that you *can*. In the previous chapter I encouraged you to throw out the traditional rulebook when it comes to workwear style; let's replace those indeterminate rules with eight guidelines to help you to get started in selecting what to wear; nothing complicated, just the basic building blocks.

1. Consider whose style you find inspiring

Who are your role models? Be influenced by them, but don't copy their looks slavishly.

My style role models are (unoriginally) Audrey Hepburn and Grace Kelly. The late Carolyn Bessette-Kennedy is another source of inspiration and I love the Duchess of Cambridge's recent looks, too. The easy elegance and graceful demeanour of all four women influences the styles I favour. Of course, there's no way I am seeking to emulate their perfection or wear literal copies of their clothes. I'm a 21st-century businesswoman, parliamentarian and campaigner with a generous but limited wardrobe budget, not a beautiful 1950s' Hollywood actress, American fashion publicist and socialite or future queen with a team of ladies-in-waiting, stylists, dressmakers and protocol experts on hand. Your stylistic role models might be similarly unobtainable or they might be close friends or women you work with – the key is to be inspired, not a wannabe.

In any case, none of my role models actually offer career-dressing templates: they offer general guidance around the art of dressing well. When I shop for an outfit I'm looking for something that works for my life, while being drawn towards flattering fit-and-flare dresses and narrow coats (the Duchess of Cambridge), sleek minimalist shapes (Carolyn Bessette-Kennedy), shirt-dresses, slim ankle-length trousers and classic polo necks (Audrey Hepburn) and chic separates for daytime plus glorious chiffon for special occasions (Princess Grace). Certain looks do give me specific ideas: my all-time favourite 'Princess Kate' outfit is a pale blue diaphanous skirt and blouse by Lebanese designer Elie Saab, which the Duchess wore at Royal Ascot in 2019 with a matching hat and silver heels. Her beautiful tulle concoction would not translate well to the office, but the soft blue colour certainly does. I kept a lookout and found a simple shift dress by Roland Mouret in the exact same shade that's perfect for work. (Confession: I loved her actual Ascot dress so much that I also tracked down a much less expensive version by Costarellos to wear to a wedding or party. I'm not usually a copycat, but every now and again something justifies it!)

When I study looks worn by the women who inspire me, it's often the smaller details that translate most literally into my own wardrobe: Grace Kelly's silk scarves and structured top-handle bags; Audrey Hepburn's minimalist approach to jewellery; Carolyn Bessette-Kennedy's ultra-simple necklines; the Duchess's sharp high-heeled pumps. I did buy a replica of

Grace Kelly's overnight case from *Rear Window* (the original makers, Mark Cross, reissued the bag). I ordered it online and hadn't realised quite how small it was! There's barely room for a toothbrush and change of underwear, let alone a nightdress. But I decided to keep it, and every time someone compliments me on it (that bag garners a lot of attention) I tell them that I actually bought it as an overnight case – to much incredulity and laughter.

There is so much choice – at every price point. Your style queens can help you to decide what you like and to edit accordingly. If in doubt, I do find myself wondering: *would Audrey Hepburn wear this?* But sometimes, even if the answer is no, I'll go ahead. What works today differs from when she was on the silver screen – and I don't want to look as if I'm stuck in a time warp. Remember, whoever your style icons are, you are your own person, living your own life. Let them guide but not restrict you.

2. Think about the physical characteristics you like about yourself

Qualified praise – 'my hair isn't too awful' – doesn't count. Only *unequivocal* positives are allowed. Although it feels uncomfortably like boasting, I'm going to say it: I like being slim. Clothes that skim my body are most flattering. Anything tight accentuates my lack of curves and makes me feel uncomfortable (both physically and mentally), but I mustn't shroud my best feature in shapeless or oversized clothes. On the occasions I've done so, I felt nondescript, and that's a miserable backdrop to what might otherwise be a good day at work.

Your best feature might be beautiful hair, unusual colouring, great eyes, shapely legs – or simply being well proportioned. Almost every woman has something special about her, and if not, it's usually because she is hiding it. My friend Liz Dimmock, in her early forties, is a keen cyclist with an athletic build. She is founder and CEO of Moving Ahead, a social enterprise that runs mentoring programmes, including the 30% Club's cross-company mentoring scheme, the largest in the world. At the big events for Moving Ahead, Liz usually wears a neat fitted dress that shows off her great legs. My former colleague CJ Fildes, in her late twenties, has beautiful blonde hair. She often wears it up 'to be taken seriously', but her hair looks gorgeous that way as well as worn loose. CJ's go-to work outfit is a LBD (little black dress), because she knows that works so well with her blonde hair. Political commentator and fund-raiser Sarah Elliott, 39, is a classic hourglass shape. She's happy to wear clothes that show her figure 'without showing everything off'. Presenter and director of creative diversity at the BBC, June Sarpong, always wears great lipstick that draws attention to her fabulous smile. Each and every woman is working with, rather than hiding, her best assets, enhancing her presence.

3. Take time to understand your body shape

Dressing for your body shape helps to project a more con-sidered look, in turn boosting your confidence and making you feel comfortable and in control – all positive factors at work. We might find it hard to assess ourselves accurately. I've some-times veered off-course and been tempted to dress as if I have a curvy hourglass figure, or in colours that would work well on tanned blondes. In reality, I am what is bluntly described as a 'column' – narrow, straight up and down – with naturally auburn-brown hair (well, naturally in my youth), pale skin and freckles. To look and feel the best version of myself, I need clothes that give me the illusion of shape and to avoid colours that wash me out (either because they are too insipid or too overwhelming).

We'll come on to colours shortly, but let's spend a few moments considering your body shape. This exercise might feel like taking a quiz in a teenage magazine, but it might also explain why some outfits never feel quite right, whereas others feel – and look – great. Some guides suggest that there are as many as 12 different categories for women, but that's over-complicating things. Style is not a science. Most of us fall roughly into one of the following five types. Take a look at the drawings and see which most closely approximates your figure.

The Column – as it sounds, straight up and down with similar-sized hips and bust, and a trim waist, but few curves. If you're like me, also rather flat-chested. You aren't necessarily tall: the Duchess of Cambridge and Gwyneth Paltrow (both five feet nine/1.75m) are columns, but so is Natalie Portman, who's just five feet three (1.60m).

The Triangle or Pear – narrower shoulders than hips, defined waist, curvy hips and thighs, narrow shoulders, slim arms, a smaller bust. Kim Kardashian and Jennifer Lopez are both 'curvy' pears; Keira Knightley is a very slender version.

The Inverted Triangle – broader shoulders than hips with less waist definition. Slim legs and a sporty-looking physique are often associated with this body shape. Model Naomi Campbell and actress Cameron Diaz have this body shape, with strong shoulders and narrow hips.

The Hourglass – the classic curvy feminine shape, with similar dimensions around the hips and bust, and a small waist. There are 'full' hourglasses with voluptuous proportions and 'neat' hourglasses. Actresses Penelope Cruz, Halle Berry, Scarlett Johansson and Salma Hayek all have hourglass figures.

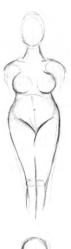

The Apple – a more rounded torso (although this needn't mean actually round), with less waist definition than the hourglass, well-proportioned bust and hips – often with lovely legs. Catherine Zeta-Jones, Drew Barrymore and Liz Hurley are apples, proving that this shape can be very slim.

Identifying our body shape shouldn't make us feel limited about what to wear, but it can help us select from the vast range of style choices. I see now that I tended to wear baggy clothes for much of my twenties, partly because I was too thin to find things that fitted well, but also because oversized and unstructured jackets were fashionable at the time. I didn't feel great in my clothes, and that didn't help me feel great at work. Some days I was literally over-whelmed by what I was wearing. That undermined my confidence, and I tended to hold back. On the days when I wore something more flattering I would feel happier and found it easier to speak up: I had a short, fitted navy jacket paired with a soft floral knee-length skirt – the outfit suited my shape and struck a balance between classic workwear (the jacket) and a girly look (the skirt). Now I know to simply give a trend a miss if it doesn't suit me.

Choosing clothes for your shape

Here are some ideas about what might work on your particular shape. They might just confirm what you already know even if you haven't thought about it in this way before. You'll see a pattern if you read through all the different types – the suggestions all help to create balance and a well-proportioned shape, whatever your underlying figure. For work clothes, which of course is the em-phasis here, a general principle applies: you'll look more elegant and feel comfortable when clothes are cut to skim not cling.

The Column

Styling goals It's all about creating a little curve.

It's easy to create the illusion of shape, starting with defining the waist. As a column, I tend to choose styles with a waistband, or I'll use a belt to draw in dresses. The most flattering jackets are fitted but not too skimpy. Ideally, they curve out towards the hip and have structured shoulders to create a little more width. The jacket is hourglass, even though I'm not. I've just returned a beautiful cream jacket bought online because it is not fitted enough to do me any favours. The best dresses have a close-fitting top, then flare out to a fuller skirt. Loose all over just drowns this shape, but tightly fitted emphasises the lack of curves. A simple shift can work if you want to create a neat, slim silhouette. Think of how the Duchess of Cambridge dresses in a body-conscious way, but nothing too constricting. Although it's clearly not suitable for work, I've learned about flattering shapes from the compliments I get when wearing my favourite party dress. It's a strapless shimmery column with big pleated sections at one hip and at the opposite side of the neckline – which might sound weird but creates an amazing illusion of curves. I'm always on the lookout for daytime versions. I've also learned that certain necklines are good at creating width where it's needed: boat necks, cut wide from shoulder to shoulder, suit this shape well. (Think of the Duchess of Sussex's beautifully austere wedding dress.)

Less flattering Dropped waistlines, double-breasted, bulky or shapeless jackets. Anything shaped like a sack – but also steer clear of anything too clingy.

The Triangle or Pear

Styling goals Balance out your silhouette by creating more volume on your top half, drawing attention to your slim waist and de-emphasising your bottom half.

Structured shoulders will widen the shoulder line to balance it with your hips. If you'd rather not wear a jacket, flowing blouses work well, again giving more bulk at the top. Necklaces, scarves and interesting collars can all create volume where you need it most – they also make your existing wardrobe more versatile. Gently flared dresses (wrap dresses can work brilliantly), skirts and belts that define and emphasise the waist work best. Simple, straight tapered skirts that fall to or below the knee are another fail-safe option (just make sure that they aren't too tight around your hips). Well-cut tailored trousers are flattering. Wearing brighter colours or patterns on your top half and darker plain colours on your bottom half is another good trick. Oscar-winning actress Kate Winslet dresses more for the red carpet than the office, but her tendency to emphasise her shoulders is spot on for all pear shapes. TV presenter Naga Munchetty is a trim version of this shape; again, she wears dresses and jackets that broaden her shoulder line. In a photo shoot for *Vogue* magazine Naga looked amazing in a Victoria Beckham structured jacket and slim flowing trousers, all in glorious rich tones.

Less flattering Tight pencil skirts or mini-skirts that end at a wide point on your legs, boxy dresses that hide your defined waist.

The Inverted Triangle

Styling goals To balance out your top and bottom halves, drawing attention to slim hips and legs while softening the shoulder line.

You are looking for styles that add curves to the hips and bottom, and define your waist while de-emphasising your top half. Soft-shouldered jackets that extend beyond the hips, tops with narrow V- or U-shaped necklines, and well-tailored wide-legged trousers create balance. Wearing lighter colours or patterns on your lower half, and plain darker colours on top, is another simple trick. Slim pencil skirts and skinny trousers will emphasise your slender hips (you might decide this is something you wish to emphasise rather than to hide) and shorter skirts will show off your legs. Charlene, Princess of Monaco and former Olympic swimmer is a very clear example of an inverted triangle shape, with strong broad shoulders. Soft-shouldered suits are some of her best looks, along with high-waisted trousers and jumpsuits. Actress and humanitarian Angelina Jolie is a very slim inverted triangle shape. When she received her honorary damehood from the Queen, she wore a beautiful dove-grey suit, again with a softly cut jacket. For evening wear, both women tend to favour strapless dresses, showing off their toned shoulders without adding extra bulk.

Less flattering Structured broad-shouldered jackets, big scarves, wide necklines, patterns or frills on top, very tight skirts.

The Hourglass

Styling goals To highlight your small waist and ideal feminine shape without being too provocative.

The hourglass pretty much has every option to choose from, apart from shapeless or bulky styles that hide your waist. This shape is perfect for form-fitting, tailored clothing, which works in so many settings. A fitted blouse and skirt with a defined waistline or a close-fitting dress all work well. Fitted does not mean tight! That's especially true for a more voluptuous hourglass shape, like my friend Sarah Elliott. Sarah has always been conscious of not attracting the 'wrong sort of attention' and the extra hurdles involved in being taken seriously, especially with long blonde hair. She remembers a female 'mentor' abruptly telling her early in her career to 'find clothes that fit' when she'd worn a shirt that was just a little too tight – a comment that knocked her confidence. That advice should have been shared more gently and kindly. Sarah now uses a tailor so that she can buy trousers,

jackets and shirts that fit well over her curves, especially a generous bust, and then has the waists nipped in and darts added,
particularly for those tricky button-through shirts, which have
a habit of gaping across the chest. She also loves shift dresses to
create a neat line and skim over curves, where she doesn't have
to worry about tugging or gaping. Sarah also recommends classic
A-line skirts worn with neat tops to draw attention to a slim waist
(noting that her 'favourite designer of all time has to be Dior'),
solid colours and V-necks. She will use a necklace, scarf or blazer
to create the illusion of a V-neck on crew-necked shifts.

Less flattering Boxy or double-breasted jackets, overly tight
clothes, patterns (too distracting), pleats (too bulky).

The Apple

Styling goals To create balanced proportions, the impression of a
shapely waist and highlighting your slim hips and legs.

The most flattering styles for you depend on whether you are a
rounded or a slim apple. Rounded shapes will look best in styles
that skim over the waist; slimmer apples will benefit from creating
the illusion of a smaller waist with styles that are fitted around the
middle. That cream jacket I just returned would look great on a
more rounded apple. It's cut to gently skate over the waist and has a
beautiful simple collar and buttons that draw the eye. Simple shifts
can look really lovely and elegant on more generously proportioned
apples, again skimming the body, showing just the right amount of
leg. And they are versatile, too. Different colours and fabrics can
create quite distinct looks suitable for a variety of situations, and
you can add jackets, cardigans or matching coats to create strong
statement looks where the occasion calls. My daughter-in-law
Dyedra is a petite apple shape; she loves 1950s' style dresses for

special occasions to create a small waist, and simple jackets (again, no extra fabric around the middle) and shorter pencil skirts or tailored high-waisted trousers for work that flatter her slim hips and legs. Catherine Zeta-Jones wore an elegant cream outfit and hat when she collected her CBE from Prince Charles. The single-button jacket created a very slim line through the waist, paired with a simple matching shift dress. In general, choose soft fabrics so that you avoid unwanted bulk around the stomach and bust.

Less flattering Double-breasted jackets and anything that involves any excess fabric in the middle of your body. Be careful with waistlines that they don't add extra bulk, low-rise trousers that put the emphasis in exactly the wrong place, and longer length skirts that obscure your legs.

Strategies for distinct shapes and sizes

These are the basic body shapes. Our height and weight will obviously have a bearing on the specific styles that suit us best, along with any distinctive physical features. Janine Menaskanian is five feet nothing (1.52m), a UK size 6 with curves – and size 3 shoes! Janine has a senior role in the finance industry and is the mother of twin teenage girls. Her 'style breakthrough' came when she returned to work after having the twins and resolved to reinvigorate both her career and wardrobe. Before having children, she wore conventional suits, which were tricky to find for her size and shape, and even harder to alter to fit (especially trousers, which often lost their original proportions when cut down). Suits also demanded the right shirts – which then needed ironing. It was a lot of effort with mixed results. After having her babies, Janine sent most of her work clothes to a charity shop, paring right down to a few dresses, and found her new minimalist approach was much easier. Dresses

were simpler to alter – just a hem or sleeve length to shorten – and
she could vary the look using scarves and jewellery. Since then,
Janine has focused on finding the best brands and ideal shapes
for her body – she doesn't have much luck with petite high-street
ranges but likes French workwear brands such as Claudie Pierlot,
Maje and Sandro. Wrap dresses are perfect for her curves, and her
favourite brand for special items (including jackets for the office) is
Vivienne Westwood, because the cut accentuates her waist.

Ironically, Vivienne Westwood is also the designer of choice
for Birgit Neu, at the other end of the height spectrum at six feet
three (1.91m)! Birgit is former global head of diversity and inclusion at HSBC, born to German parents in the United States. She
'hated being tall' growing up in suburbia, but suddenly found it an
advantage when she moved to New York at 17. Queuing outside a
nightclub the crowds suddenly parted to let her in: 'people assumed
I was *somebody* because I was so tall'. When Birgit started working in finance she found herself 'at eye level' with those tall male
executives: a distinct advantage. And clothes shopping wasn't 'too
terrible' in New York – many affordable brands ran longer length
versions of their regular sizes. When Birgit moved to London aged
33, there was a dearth of options. At one point when she 'literally
had nothing to wear to the office', colleagues suggested she try
Savile Row, the famous street in Mayfair known for its bespoke
menswear. Birgit started at No. 1, Gieves & Hawkes, founded in
1771. 'I walked in by myself and the salesman looked at me like I
was from another planet. I explained my problem; he reluctantly
mulled it over and brought up a woman from their basement
who took pity on me and offered to make me trousers.' And so
Birgit began a long friendship with Kathryn Sargent, who became
Gieves & Hawkes' head cutter, the first woman to do so in the
history of Savile Row before opening her own atelier, which offers
both classic gentlemen's tailoring and womenswear.

In common with everyone I've spoken with who has a 'size challenge' (whatever that is), Birgit has developed a strategy. She always carries spare clothes in her hand luggage when travelling on business, for example, knowing that if her checked-in bag goes astray, she won't be able to just run to the closest shop and buy something that fits. She makes a note of the labels worn by the tallest celebrities on social media and explores those. She is also creative about alterations: she loved a beautiful coat that was long enough but the sleeves were too short, so she ended up having extended cuffs sewn on in a contrasting fabric. If midi-skirts are fashionable, she'll stock up that season; when shorter hemlines are in she'll just sit it out. And given the high cost of specially made or altered items, she'll save her money for those stand-out pieces that make her feel great for important work occasions, donning an inexpensive black high-street dress for every day, upgraded and varied with jewellery and accessories that work for all shapes and sizes. Despite the practical challenges, Birgit has come to see being extra-tall – with blonde hair – as a positive; when she worked in banking there were 6,000 co-workers in the same London office yet people knew who she was. She doesn't even downplay her height with flat shoes – as she says, 'I already stand out – what's the point in trying to pretend otherwise?'

At 51, Birgit has reached the stylistic goal of becoming so confident that she chooses to exaggerate her distinct features rather than disguise them. She *owns* her looks and uses them to her advantage in business. Instagram influencer Emily Jane Johnston is both very tall (six feet two inches/1.88m) and a curvy size 18. She always looks utterly fabulous and ignores all the plus-size diktats, gleefully donning horizontal stripes, a bare midriff, mini-skirts and tutus. As Emily puts it so brilliantly, 'Style is 100 per cent a state of mind, not a size . . . at all!' She delights in busting fashion myths. Emily's confidence is infectious – I feel more self-assured just reading her posts. But, for most of us, self-belief and the development of a strong personal brand takes time and practice – especially when we are dressing for work. It's an iterative process: I can now see that I gradually developed my confidence by pushing out the frontiers of my stylistic comfort zone, discovering something that worked, feeling bolstered by the feedback and then repeating. Those boring shapeless navy suits were not replaced with colourful fit-and-flare dresses overnight, but as I embraced looks that better suited my body shape and personality, I became my own person at work, and more successful too. And dressing to suit our shape doesn't require spending a small fortune. Yes, I spent more money on my clothes as my career progressed, but a big clothes budget is neither necessary nor a guarantee of style. Happily, there are now many ways to dress beautifully and ethically on a tight budget, which we'll explore shortly.

4. Invest in well-fitting underwear

Just as you wouldn't paint a wall without preparing it first, good underwear can make all the difference to the fit of an outfit, and to your comfort and posture. Get it right and that's one less thing to worry about or be distracted by during your working day. We're told that eight out of ten women are wearing the wrong bra size and although I'm not convinced we're that clueless, it's worth getting professionally measured just to check.[17] Most lingerie shops and department store concessions offer this as a free service. It's taken me a long time to find a flattering bra (that is, one that gives my modest chest some sort of shape, without looking fake, and adjustable straps – a low bust is very ageing), plus briefs that don't dig in and create visible pantie lines and tights that offer enough coverage for my very pale thread-veined legs without looking dense. You might have very different challenges; curvy Sarah Elliott is a big fan of Spanx and lesser known brand Honeylove shapewear that 'smooths everything out', as well as old-fashioned slips that make dresses (especially unlined ones) hang so much better. These days we are lucky to have many shapewear options for all sizes, skin colours and price points. Different outfits might require specific underwear; again, just try things on *before* you need to head out the door, and look in a full-length mirror. It's worth investing in a mirror that's both tall enough to let you see your outfit from top to toe and wide enough to give a sense of how you appear in a room. That way you'll have a better idea of how others will see you than if you just see an isolated reflection, which can be distorting. Ideally, your mirror should be free-standing, tilted back against the wall – again this gives a more realistic picture – and placed in natural or good lighting. That quick check in the mirror has often revealed that I don't look quite as I'd intended because my underwear is wrong: a bra strap is visible or there are lumps and bumps around my waist and hips. Investment bank UBS might have been mocked for their insistence that female employees wear flesh-coloured underwear, but it is often the safest option for the office. (Although I know some people hate the look of nude underwear. If that includes you, choose a colour that appeals more but doesn't show.)

My favourite lingerie brand is Stella McCartney – a perfect fit, long lasting and (in the styles I choose) invisible – closely followed by lesser-known Chantelle, which has a good range of seamless bras, briefs and camisoles. I am also big fan of Kim Kardashian's Skims for surprisingly comfortable shapewear – and it comes in every shade of 'nude'. And here's my review of different hosiery brands based on a widely held preference among working women for nearly invisible, matt tights. I've rated them according to a number of criteria, including price, range of colours offered, ability to stay up (!), texture and durability.

Hosiery review

Brand	Price	Colour (true nude)	Colour (range)	Stay-up power	Texture	Durability	Invisibility	Fit/control	Overall score
Heist The Nude	1 (£21.00)	5	5 (7 shades)	5	4	5	4 (slightly thick but seamless around hips/waist)	5 (no seam, amazing!)	34
M&S Autograph Invisible Bodyshaper 7 denier appearance	4 (£6.00)	3 (slightly grey)	3 (3 shades)	5	4	5	4	4	32
Falke Shelina 12	3 (£11.00)	4	5 (8 shades)	3	5	1	5	3	29
M&S Autograph Ladder Resist 7 denier appearance	5 (£7 for 2 pairs)	3 (slightly grey)	2 (2 shades)	5	3 (slightly shiny)	4	3 (spoilt by visible reinforced toe)	4	29
Wolford Luxe 9 Control top	3 (£23)	4	5 (8 shades)	3	4	3	5	4 (good control top but with seam)	29
Falke Invisible Deluxe 8	3 (£11.75)	4	5 (6 shades)	3	4	2	4	3	28
Wolford Individual 10 Control Top	0 (£35)	4	5 (7 shades)	3	3 (slightly thick)	4	4	4 (good control but with seam)	27
John Lewis 10 denier (3 pairs)	5 (£5 for 3)	2 (too grey)	3 (3 skintone shades)	3	3	3	3 (visible reinforced toe)	4	26
Wolford Nude 8	1 (£19)	4 (gobi is my favourite)	5 (7 shades)	2 (keep falling down)	4	2 (very sheer)	5	3 (saggy round legs)	26
Snagtights Sheer 30 Denier	4 (£7)	2 (grey tone)	3 (3 shades)	4	2 (too thick)	3	3	5 (huge range of sizes)	26
Spanx Sheers	1 (£22.50)	1 (too grey)	2 (2 shades)	2	2	3	3	3	17

Key: 0–5 ratings for the different criteria, where 0 is the worst score and 5 the best

5. Wear the right colours for your skin tone and colouring

Carefully chosen colours that are right for you will lift your spirits (as well as those around you) and help to create a positive impact, both in the office and online. Stylist Annie Castaño helps people 'look like themselves' by identifying their best colour palette and style personality.[18] Annie declares, 'Get the colours right and you look vibrant, welcoming, friendly and people concentrate on what you are saying. Get them wrong and your clothes become a distraction, off-putting, ageing and you look unwell.' Over the years, I've simply used a mirror to try to work out which colours are best for me (my family is also good at sharing candid opinions when something doesn't work), but having our colours 'done' professionally can save time and money in the long run and identify more quickly the colours that make us look and feel great. Annie showed me (over Zoom) the contrast between getting colours right and wrong. She held swathes of fabric up to her face: the right colours made her come alive; the wrong colours made her look washed-out. Annie categorises people into one of four main colour groups, denoted by the seasons; she is 'autumn', so warm, soft colours enhance her natural colouring. Even two different shades of mid-blue – one with yellow undertones, the other an electric blue – had dramatically different effects. The first lifted and brightened her face, the second had the opposite effect. I wondered if she had changed the lighting in the room – but it was the colour of the fabric that changed the way the light fell on her face. If you have ever seen colour illusions (like the famous image of a stripy dress that went viral as people argued over whether it was blue and black or white and gold), you'll know that the same colours can look very different – and different colours can look surprisingly similar. One major determinant of how we see colours is the context: the other colours around them. When a colour is put next to your face, it will influence the way others will see you. Annie goes as far as to say that colour does '70 per cent of the work for you' when it comes to presenting yourself in the best way for work. Again, it's tremendously empowering to discover what works.

Some people have very clear-cut colouring. My daughter, Octavia, is an obvious 'winter': cool and bright. She has very dark brown hair, pale skin (even in summer, when she just gets a sprinkling of freckles) and clear blue-green eyes with striking dark eyebrows. She looks wonderful in strong colours: scarlet, emerald green, rich purple, cobalt blue, and both black and pure white suit her, too. Pastel shades don't flatter her at all. Her younger sister, Cecily, also has dark brown hair, but is a 'spring': soft and bright. Her skin tans easily and she has light green eyes. She looks lovely in peachy shades, soft yellow, green and blue. Pastels generally flatter her, some brights work well (orange is good when she has a tan) but strong purple and red are overwhelming. Their older sister Florence is a 'summer': cool and soft. Sky blue, cornflower, jade and lavender – the colour she chose as her wedding theme – all look wonderful on her. You might be on the cusp of two different seasons; it's less a matter of being fixated by the label and more about knowing the colours that suit you. Those who've had their colours analysed in this way receive a sample book of their best shades, making shopping a lot simpler.

If we don't seek an expert's opinion, we can obviously still work out what suits us, partly based on the feedback. I tend to get compliments wearing certain colours and 'Are you OK? You look rather tired' comments wearing others, which makes it rather obvious. I know that my colouring is fairly easy to dress, with a good range of choices, but a few colours look awful. Those include most shades of beige and grey (I look washed out), neon colours (overwhelming at my age, although I'm still tempted to wear hot pink and bright orange, carefully) and unless I'm wearing extra make-up I just can't wear black – even though I love its sophistication and enjoy wearing black in summer with a slight tan. I once bought a lovely skirt suit in a pale duck-egg blue that made me look ill. I wore it to an investment conference and then changed into a more flattering colour for the evening session – interestingly, someone introduced himself to me who I been working with during the day, not recognising me at all! I now steer away from anything in that colour, even if I love the style. To help you see things objectively, ask a friend, sister or someone whose opinion you trust (in my case my daughters are very helpful) to go through your existing wardrobe with you, holding the fabric of each dress, top or jacket up close to your face and agreeing which colours bring your face alive and any that have the opposite effect. There will be some that aren't an obvious hit or miss. Honesty is key. Don't stress if you have lots of items in the 'wrong' colours: they can usually be made to work by wearing accessories such as scarves or necklaces, or a jacket or cardigan – something near your face – in a more flattering shade. I found a combination of a creamy pearl necklace and ivory-based silk scarf made even the duck-egg suit wearable, although I have to admit to feeling relieved when it came back damaged from the dry-cleaner's and I could move on.

If your job is 'corporate' rather than 'creative', conventional wisdom says that you should pick one or two colours from the neutral palette of navy, grey, black and camel to give a favoured base for items such as coats, shoes and bags, more conservative dresses, jackets and other stalwarts of your career wardrobe. We're aiming to push the boundaries here. The ultimate goal is that you dress in a way that enables you to be the best version of yourself. Hopefully *you* get to decide whether that is in navy blue or pink. But we also recognise that some sectors and companies aren't there yet – and you might want to push out those boundaries slowly. Traditional 'serious' colours can help you feel comfortable while you build up your own confidence and credentials. And even within the narrow confines of dark colours you can still pick shades that suit you best. Choose between black, charcoal, dark brown, navy, perhaps even the darkest forest green and deepest burgundy. Having a preferred basic shade also helps to make a small wardrobe go further since everything will work well together. Make up your mind about white, ivory or cream. Pure white can be harsh (especially on Zoom) but works well if you are a 'winter' colourway; creamy ivory suits me better as a brightener to an otherwise sombre outfit on grey English days. If you are going with a more traditional palette, choose a few accents: they could be stronger base colours such as red or cobalt blue, or shades that you feel more comfortable limiting to a 'pop' of colour, such as fuchsia. Remember, again, these are not strict rules (unless you're a purist). Being aware of your most flattering colours will help you to edit and feel confident about your choices. You don't have to stick rigidly to your ideal palette. If you come across a perfect-fitting, potentially very useful dress in a different colour (but not one on the 'avoid at all costs' list) consider whether it suits you enough in other respects and if you can make the colour work for you by adding a scarf or bold jewellery. Annie has collaborated with an artist, Ivana Nohel, to create scarves in the different colour seasons that bring the best colours closest to your face, and are especially useful for Zoom.[19]

Finally, a reminder that this isn't an academic exercise. I've just seen pictures of Nimco Ali, indefatigable campaigner against female genital mutilation, alongside a newspaper interview about her work. She's photographed in bright pink and lime-green

prints (adorned with flowers as well) and looks fabulous. Those
are potentially difficult colours to wear – yet it's obvious to
anyone who sees the pictures that they work brilliantly on her.
She looks commanding yet feminine. A woman whose opinion
you would want to hear. Modern feminists wear pink!

6. Think about your favourite clothes

In this context, I'm excluding pyjamas, sportswear, swimwear,
ball gowns or jeans – unless your workplace permits them. Which
outfits make your feel great? Take a careful look and consider
what it is that makes them work for you. I feel at my best in
dresses: they make me feel put-together and I find them easy to
style. A newspaper once suggested that my predilection for simple
designer dresses was because they were effectively glorified 'one-
sies'! I don't avoid trouser suits, it's just that dresses are my go-to.
Skirt suits now tend to make me feel frumpy: Yasmin Le Bon took
the words out of my mouth when she told *Stella* magazine, 'The
only thing I can't do at 56 is *granny chic* – it's no longer ironic.'

As we've already established, my favourite dresses tend to
share similarities: they have a fit-and-flare shape, they might be
an interesting colour, skim rather than cling, fall below the knee,
are often short-sleeved or are sleeveless. If you looked through
my wardrobe, you'd see mainly variations on these themes. Each
dress is distinct, but they also look as though they belong to
the same person (there are no bohemian styles for example, few
prints and the colour palette is consistent). I feel happy when I
open my wardrobe, confident that I'll find something to work for
whatever lies ahead – including accommodating my mood and
the weather, even if neither is very good that day! It's evening
as I'm writing this, and I've been thinking about what to wear

tomorrow. I have several online meetings, both formal and less so, I'm conducting a live interview with a Member of Parliament as part of a webinar, and I have to catch up on admin. I'll take Bea to school and will go for a walk or two with our dog Buddy, so I'll need to change quickly. I don't want to spend too much time on my outfit. I opened the wardrobe and quickly found a dress that works for the various aspects of the work day. It's 'wow' enough for the webinar but not over the top for the informal meetings. Given that I'll be working from home, I don't even need to find the shoes that work with it. Finding your style makes your life easier.

7. Regularly maintain your clothes

Set aside a time each month to organise, edit, clean, alter and repair your clothes.

At this stage in my life, I have amassed a rather large collection, so I frequently review the clothes that make me feel at my best and work for now. Those pieces go to the front of my wardrobe. If something is never going to work (after a while we have to face the reality of a mistaken purchase, or acknowledge we're past the age to carry off a certain look), I gift it to one of my six daughters or to charity or remodel it. After analysing their colours, Annie Castaño helps women 'detox' their wardrobes. She has clients in their sixties who have held on to pieces last worn at university. Unless something carries a special memory, find another home for items you are not going to wear. Even if we don't hoard, storage is often an issue. Keep a lookout for storage solutions to help organise your clothes and accessories – it might take a little imagination. These days I can locate my various pairs of shoes easily: when we bought our house the one item of furniture we purchased from the previous owner was an old cabinet in a small alcove at the top of the stairs – a space that would otherwise have ended up being used for clutter. The cabinet has perfectly shoe-box-sized drawers – 32 of them! I posted a picture on Instagram and the mystery was solved: it's an old draper's shop display cabinet made by D. & A. Binder. The history is fascinating, the cabinet very practical.

Most of us have some items of clothing that don't fit. We might have gained or lost weight, or perhaps they never felt quite right. Alterations can seem expensive but are usually much less so, and less wasteful, than making another purchase. Try your local dry-cleaner for straightforward, low-cost alterations. If you have something special, perhaps a precious hand-me-down or second-hand find that was obviously intended for someone else's body, you may need an expert tailor. I've discovered a wonder-ful (London-based) company, the Wardrobe Curator, and, as a result of their magic, I now regularly wear several outfits that had previously hung unworn, making me feel guilty every time I looked at them. They even slimmed down a jacket (which seemed impossible) and took in trousers to transform a suit that had hung droopily off me. It's since become one of my favourites. My mother, who's in her eighties and always very elegant, has found a local dressmaker in her Sussex town who's happy to undertake alterations. If you can't find anyone close to where you live, ask friends and neighbours for recommendations. There are sewing tasks that we can manage ourselves: if you discover a hem coming undone, or a tiny hole, repair it as soon as you can. I met Beth Salmen on a photoshoot for *Brummell*, a lifestyle magazine for professionals working in London's financial district. Beth, in her thirties, always looks polished yet creative, as befits her role as an advertising executive. She says she doesn't need many clothes, preferring separates that can be mixed and matched to create interesting and thoughtful looks, but she *insists* that everything is scrupulously clean and well looked after. Moths are the scourge of many a wardrobe. After losing some treasured items to them, I have a slight obsession with both prevention (follow Beth's example and keep your clothes clean, and hang cedar-wood blocks or lavender bags in your wardrobe) and cure (break the cycle using pheromone moth traps; the Wardrobe Curator also sells a fantastic non-toxic chrysanthemum-based moth-killer spray which smells surprisingly good). If your wardrobe is basically well organised, you'll only need to set aside an hour or so a month to maintain it (plus clothes cleaning), but it will be an hour well spent and save you both time and money in the long run.

8. Be realistic about your budget, and shop consciously

Over-spending will lead to other stresses. Fortunately, we now have a number of options to make our hard-earned money go further *and* avoid cluttering up the planet. My former colleague CJ is dubbed the eBay Queen by her friends. She has set herself two specific rules: not to buy anything she'll only wear once, and not to buy at full price. (She's making an exception on both counts for her wedding dress.) There are many great sources of vintage and nearly new (or never worn) clothes available at a fraction of their original prices. My eldest daughter enjoys finding new homes for her own treasured pieces 'so their story may continue' via her 'Florence Clementine Archive' Instagram feed. Flo takes great pleasure in wrapping everything beautifully and sending the items off all around the world, and even more delight when the new owner sends a photograph of herself looking wonderful in them. If you're looking for regular second-hand style inspiration, Charlotte Stella, a 23-year-old law student, has a fabulous Instagram account, @stellar_charlotte, where she displays charity shop finds from Oxfam, Royal Trinity Hospice and Amnesty UK, along with items from Depop and eBay. Other students on a tight budget might take the easy fast fashion route; Charlotte told me that her grandparents first introduced her to second-hand style, having grown up during the war when clothes rationing encouraged everyone to 'make do and mend'. They played a significant role in her upbringing: Charlotte is a triplet and her father left the family when she was little, leaving her mother to work full-time while battling a chronic autoimmune disease. When she was old enough to make her own wardrobe choices Charlotte 'carried on raiding relatives' wardrobes' and exploring charity shops. Not only is Charlotte determined to shop sustainably and ethically; she also confesses to having 'quite expensive taste for someone on a tight budget', which fast fashion doesn't live up to. As an aspiring lawyer, she's looking to create a quality professional wardrobe: charity shops mean she can afford to buy better for less. She offers some great advice for sourcing second-hand clothes: 'I use magazines, Pinterest and Instagram to create "wish lists" of sorts, and so I always go into charity shops with a rough idea of the sort of pieces I'm looking for. This helps me to avoid impulse purchases and hold out for items that I really love.'

'Pre-loved' might not appeal to you, but sustainability concerns demand that we rethink fast fashion. We've become more conscious about waste, climate change and worker conditions, especially during the pandemic. In 2020, the number of online searches for sustainable fashion increased by a sizeable 37 per cent.[20] It's not necessarily obvious which brands are leading and lagging when it comes to ethical issues, so we need to do our homework. I use the excellent 'Good On You' app, which rates individual brands according to three measures: how they treat their people, the environment, and animals. Sadly, many familiar and popular brands score poorly. Fast fashion may seem cheap but it comes at a high hidden cost. The year 2020's Transparency Index, a system created by Fashion Revolution, ranks brands simply on the basis of how much *information* they provide about aspects of their business including supply chains, workers' rights and manufacturing processes. Encouraging more disclosure is a good place to start. Positive Luxury is another useful resource for checking out the ethical credentials of a narrower range of designer labels. It awards a prestigious 'butterfly mark' to those that meet high standards, and it recognises that companies take their own approach to ethics and sustainability. Every rating includes a listing of each brand's specific positive actions, giving helpful extra detail behind the accreditation. The only drawback is that the labels rated by Positive Luxury are, as the name suggests, luxurious and therefore expensive.

Affordable and ethical clothing

The holy grail is well-priced, ethical, sustainable, accessible *and desirable* clothing. My teenage daughters love Reformation, a brand that prides itself on its environmental credentials. The company's slogan is genius: 'Being naked is the #1 most sustainable option. We're #2.' Their designs tend to be more suitable for a young woman's summer fun than workwear, but I check the website from time to time and have found modest dresses suitable even for me. Inevitably, the clothes cost more money than fast fashion, but they are less expensive than designer labels. It's worth investing some effort researching a few brands that work for your purse, ethics and taste – you can then save time by checking these out first when you're shopping. New sustainable brands are emerging all the time, which is exciting. Keep an eye on the ethical-brands website, Good On You, for articles about labels specialising in different styles and for a variety of budgets. They have just published a 'slow fashion' feature, for example. The way forward, as with so many things, involves thinking *differently* about the problem rather than making slight adaptations. The price of a dress from 'eco-conscious, affordable' brand Nobody's Child ranges from £32 to £45. Most of the collection is made from the same fabric, a certified sustainable viscose, and the dresses don't have zips, buttons or embellishments. They are also only available online. All these measures keep the costs down. Misha Nonoo is the founder of an eponymous workwear brand. Misha talked me through her innovative and award-winning business model. She doesn't do seasonal collections, she keeps a core offering online and manufactures on demand, reducing waste and lowering costs. Dai is another fabulous brand for work clothes, set up by a former investment banker, Joanna Dai. The website (www.daiwear.com) even offers a 'shop by shape' menu with tailored suggestions for the five body shapes listed above, as well as particular challenges (tall, short, fuller bust, fuller hip, 'tummy friendly' and maternity). Dai clothes are designed for 'elegant performance', putting comfort first and minimising environmental impact, including a recycled collection using a regenerated yarn.

These newer brands are pushing the envelope. Our favourite established brands might be dragging their feet, however, creating a dilemma. My 20-something daughters are fans of & Other Stories, a Swedish brand (owned by H&M), which tends to have a tight edit rather than endless racks of similar garments. It's rated 'It's a start' by Good On You, scoring well in some areas, poorly in others, and we're keeping an eye on how the rating evolves. Many well-known brands are making an effort to improve their sustainability rankings as the pressure from customers mounts. Zara, for example, is rated 'Not good enough', but when browsing online I was pleasantly surprised to read the fabric details for a lovely white shirtdress: 'This fibre is made from recycled PET plastic, like that used in water bottles. By transforming this waste into a new resource, we reduce the production of virgin raw materials and the consumption of water, energy and natural resources.' If we all shop more consciously and avoid stores associated with poor (or no) environmental policies and sweat-shop conditions for workers, manufacturers *will* operate to a better standard.

A different mindset for fashion in the 21st century

I consulted Stella McCartney, the doyenne and pioneer of ethical fashion, about how far she thinks the movement towards more responsible, sustainable fashion has come: 'It's funny to think that when I first started out 20 years ago I was considered the eco weirdo and was told I couldn't have a successful luxury label if I didn't use leather or fur. Now I see more and more brands thinking sustainably, and it's fantastic, I've longed for people to join my side. The thing is, it's no longer an option. It's a necessity because our house is on fire. Fashion has typically been extractive and exploitative – of resources and of people; for example, it is responsible for 10 per cent of global carbon emissions, the majority of textiles go to landfill and it's estimated that a single pair of jeans uses up to 20,000 litres of water in the creation process. We have to come together and act now, because it's not only what the customers are now demanding but what Mother Nature demands.

'You know, the fashion industry has been working with the same set of ten materials for hundreds of years, mainly because it's easy to keep using those materials which are typically unsustainable, such as leather, and not question them, but at Stella

McCartney we question everything, we are trying to show the industry that material innovation should be embraced and the tremendous benefits it brings to the planet. We have been measuring our impacts and used these insights to source more responsible materials such as organic cotton, recycled or upcycled materials, forest-friendly fibres, developing our own farm-level projects and championing innovations that have the potential to reimagine and reinvent the way we do fashion.

'We also believe that the future of fashion is circular: it will be restorative and regenerative by design and the clothes we love never end up as waste. As we continue to push boundaries and challenge the status quo we want to evolve from just reducing our impact to making a positive impact. We want to completely reimagine the fashion industry as we know it and move to a new circular economy, but altering this linear system demands radical transformation. It involves everyone in the fashion industry working together with unprecedented levels of commitment and innovation, and being accountable for their actions. There are lots of positive signs that the movement is going in the right direction, but it needs to move faster and it needs to go from talking to real meaningful action.'

Given both the environmental and economic circumstances, purchases really have to earn their place in our wardrobe (realistically, renting is not such a practical option for everyday workwear, although it can be great for special occasions). Don't feel pressured into buying into the latest trend: magazines and online stores will keep tempting us with 'just in' pieces and, although being aware of what's current can inspire us to try something new, it can also distract us from building a core wardrobe. I've seen over the years that cost per wear is a better way of assessing value for money than the initial price tag. Something cheap that is never worn is poor value compared with an item that cost ten times as much that you've worn at least 20 times. If you can, save for a few investment pieces, items such as a beautiful classic handbag that will upgrade many looks and be used again and again, a well-cut jacket and shoes that are both chic and comfortable, and help you look and feel powerful (the right shoes can encourage you to walk tall, feel confident and be taken more seriously – a subject we'll return to). When I was still a sixth-former, I used some of the money I'd earned doing a summer-holiday job to buy a beautiful pair of dark red shoes from Russell & Bromley. They were really completely out of my league at the time, but they transformed everything else in my wardrobe. The memory of them still makes me smile.

I love an idea shared by writer Elizabeth Day, who suggested that a garment's true worth should factor in how many compliments we receive wearing it: instead of cost per wear, a 'cost per compliment' system. Her guidance is that every compliment given translates to £5 off the original cost of the item. There are rules: compliments have to be sincere (not always easy to judge) and only one compliment is allowed per person for a particular garment. As Elizabeth points out, the brilliant thing about this compliments scale is its positivity. Instead of fretting over what something cost, it encourages us to think about the pleasure it gives.

If you tend to receive a lot of compliments, there is one catch to this system: it might lead to over-indulgence. There are ways to be disciplined when it comes to clothes shopping even if it doesn't come naturally, however. I met Dr Sundiatu Dixon-Fyle, a molecular biologist turned McKinsey consultant at a *Financial Times* breakfast discussion. She was wearing a dramatic grey dress covered in large bows, and I just had to ask her about it (the designer-style number turned out to be an ASOS bargain). Her look was both striking and perfect for work. I invited her to be a 'Friday Feature' for my daily career-dressing Instagram account and she talked me through her confident approach to workwear that increasingly draws upon her West African heritage. As well as believing that 'we need to signal through our dress that we are bringing something to the table, that we are confident in our abilities', Sundiatu is remarkably disciplined about her wardrobe, cataloguing everything she owns, then shopping on the basis of gaps. I've not managed the cataloguing part yet, but I have heeded her advice to focus on things that are missing rather than making repeat purchases. If you are like Mark Zuckerberg in wanting to wear the same clothes every day, that's fine, but for the rest of us, it can mean a full but limited wardrobe. I'm still a bit lacking in working-from-home clothes; for example, I've lots of formal clothes from my days as a full-time City executive, along with jeans for the weekend, but now I actively seek pieces that work for the life I am leading today.

Taken together, these guidelines provide a framework, helping us to find our style, edit from the vast selection on offer and make it easy to decide what to wear in the morning. You are almost ready to become your own stylist – and to have some fun with your style as well. To develop your own image, curate from the vast choice on offer and stay within budget. As model Lauren Hutton put it, 'Fashion is what you're offered four times a year . . . style is what you choose.' The starting point for making those choices is your personality, then your goals and the eight guidelines above. Together they create an understanding of the raw material you have to work with and how to make the most of your existing wardrobe. But before we bring everything together with tips for hair, make-up and accessories that enable you to feel great, own the room or the Zoom call, and look the part for the job you want, we must take a detour. We now need to consider style in everything *but* your appearance: how to project authority through the way you express yourself in person, in online meetings and through social media. Sartorial style *and* a powerful style of communication go hand in hand to create that strong personal brand that will make you feel confident and stand you in great stead over the course of your career.

Takeaways from Chapter 3

1. Be inspired, not daunted, by your style role models. You're developing a look that suits you – but do source ideas from those whose style you admire.
2. Focus on your best features. If you don't think you have any, think again. Play to those strengths.
3. Identify your body shape to help curate your choices, and dress to feel confident and comfortable.
4. Invest in well-fitting underwear – it will help you to look better and feel better, too. A full-length mirror, positioned well in good lighting, is another essential – use it!
5. Analyse the colours that are most flattering for you. Consider your workplace when selecting colours, but don't feel pressured to simply clone traditional dark masculine corporate uniforms. Push out the frontiers gradually if needs be. If you feel you must or want to dress in dark colours, don't just default to black, there might be a better shade for your colouring. Selecting your best colours will help you look and feel good and you will save time and money by avoiding mistakes.
6. Consider your favourite looks and what appeals about them. What are the recurring themes (fitted waists, specific hemlines or necklines, for example)? Use these as reference points to help you edit when shopping.

→

7. Sort your wardrobe into what you love, what doesn't work (sell or give those items away) and what can be altered (take them to a tailor, dressmaker or dry-cleaner offering this service). Put your favourite pieces at the front. Keep things clean and mended. Review every now and again – the seasons change, your mood, situation and shape might change, too. The goal is to feel happy and confident that you'll find something that works for your day when you open your closet. Tackle any storage problems – look for alcoves, shelving that can fit inside your wardrobe, containers that fit under the bed.

8. Respect your budget and consider how to make it stretch further. Respect the environment. Shop on the basis of the gaps in your wardrobe rather than buying duplicates. Assess the value of your clothes in terms of how often you wear them and the compliments that you receive.

Chapter 4

Finding Your Voice: Presenting Your Ideas and Making an Impact

'You need to learn how to select your thoughts just the same way you select your clothes every day. This is a power you can cultivate.'

Elizabeth Gilbert, best-selling author,
in Eat, Pray, Love

A confident style of dress creates a good first impression and helps get you noticed – both in person and online. It improves your chances of success, just as being unkempt would detract from them. It's a good start in building that strong personal brand. But obviously we also need to focus on the substance behind that style, especially *what* you say and *how* you say it. Unless you are a fashion model (and these days top models are as well known for their strong personalities as their looks), your views and how you present them – in whatever format – are important ingredients for a successful career.

This includes your presence on social media. As Suman Sidhu

highlighted in Chapter 2, LinkedIn is a great forum for expressing and supporting ideas you want to be associated with, as well
as making connections. I've found it a wonderful way to pub-
lish articles on 'issues of the day' that deserve more than just a
short tweet – and to get really interesting, thoughtful feedback.
As well as the genuine sharing of ideas, I love the way the platform celebrates people's work anniversaries, promotions and
new jobs. We should celebrate those achievements! LinkedIn is
also a great way to discover job opportunities and to put yourself 'out there'. Everyone should be a member. I'm a fan of active
social-media engagement: it can help you build relationships,
demonstrate and share expertise, increase your visibility, learn
new information, connect and get a sense of real views around
unfolding topics. Each platform has its own characteristics and,
of course, you don't have to be on everything – it's best to focus on
creating a network and presence on one or two. Always assume
that employers (both current and prospective) will do a sweep of
your social-media activity. See that – as Suman does – as another
opportunity to make a positive impression.

I'm often asked why I'm so active on Twitter; it's certainly a
less straightforward platform and not always constructive, but
I've found it a brilliant way to reach new audiences – including
people with very different views to mine. I started tweeting a
decade ago when the 30% Club was in its infancy and we wanted
to create momentum around the campaign. I soon discovered
that Twitter demanded more than mere reporting of activities;
ideas, opinions, engagement with followers and *humour* were
all needed to create a reaction and support. I broadened my
feed to include articles that I came across that seemed interesting and undiscovered, and shared my opinions about a wider
range of topics. As my followers have grown in number, so has
my impact. Newspapers and radio stations contact me about

tweets, I'm included in various 'top business Twitter accounts to follow' lists – and I enjoy (most of) the chats. Once you've built an engaged following, it's an easy way to get involved in discussions around topics that matter to you. One note of caution: it's easy to get carried away on Twitter. Tweets that make sense as part of a conversation can look outlandish in isolation – but overall, it's been a great way to build my personal brand and connect with people I would otherwise never meet. Instagram is considerably less contentious and, as you'll hear later, it's helped to give me a new lease of life over lockdown, as well as – once again – access to a whole new community, mainly women who all share an interest in style *and* what's going on in the world. Whatever social-media channels you decide to embrace, I'd certainly recommend doing *something* – to broaden your networks, create focal points around your interests and to build a public profile that employers will find interesting. As always, take things step by step if you're unsure; start with LinkedIn and follow people and conversations you find interesting, and start contributing only after you've developed a sense of how it works and how you'd like to get involved.

Presenting your ideas leads to recognition

It's worth the effort to broaden your networks. After all, as we've already established, being good at what you do at work isn't necessarily enough to get you promoted (and I can think of quite a few people who aren't technically great but still forge ahead). The way you present your ideas – both online and in person – can help you get the appropriate recognition. As with style of dress, you can learn techniques to help you select your thoughts, express ideas so that they resonate with whoever you are talking to, and make a positive impression. If aligned, sartorial and communication styles reinforce each other – for good or bad. I'm thinking of myself at that first job interview, with dull clothes *and* answers. Admittedly, that was 'good enough' to get the job then – although I don't think it would be today – but not to get the promotion. In contrast, the best moments of my career to date have involved more courageous speeches along with bolder outfits. Let's consider how we develop those vital in-person communication skills.

Be convincingly professional

When I think about the defining moments of my own career (both the triumphs and disasters), a critical factor was whether I operated with *grace under fire*. When I missed that first promotion, I'm afraid my knee-jerk reaction was petulant annoyance – I felt I had done everything expected of me and I let my disappointment show. There was plenty of opportunity to make up for that on the rather rocky road to the top of the next firm. There had been a number of resignations following a takeover of the company and I was offered – and I accepted – the role of chief investment officer by our new parent company. But later that same day, some of my colleagues suggested to our owners that perhaps I wasn't the best choice. Next morning, one of them told me what had happened. I was taken aback, to say the least. I asked if we could meet to discuss things. I wanted to understand how I could have misjudged the situation so badly and to decide what to do next. We all went into a room where my peers explained that they felt someone else in the team had more relevant experience for the job. We talked about it for a while. I remember being conscious of sounding very calm (although I felt anything *but*), taking the feedback on board, when one colleague suddenly spoke up. He said it was courageous of me to ask for the meeting, that I had consistently shown leadership qualities and perhaps I should be made chief executive officer instead. The others agreed ... and I walked across the street to our parent company's offices, and began with the line, 'There is a way forward', which met with a palpable sigh of relief and ready agreement to the new proposal.

I realise now that if I had become visibly upset by the initial setback, the outcome of that meeting would have been very different. It felt as if I was acting out a part, selecting the thoughts I would share, ensuring my voice was steady, my arguments remained reasoned and my credibility stayed intact. In truth, I felt vulnerable and worried. It seemed that I had little choice but to resign. But I couldn't let any of that show. I was unaware of it at the time but my performance turned into an audition for an even bigger role than the one I had hoped for, a role that was hard to reconcile with my lack of management experience. My *apparent* composure under duress made my colleagues take note.

At the time, it seemed the only possible way to react – showing how I really felt would have been too humiliating, but I was also drawing on what I'd learned through presentation skills training. The situation wasn't exactly covered by the course I'd taken, but it helped me to focus on the messages I wanted to convey, as well as my delivery. I needed to think before I spoke, control my emotions *and* create a rapport with my colleagues. Many companies offer such training; my advice is to take it if you have the opportunity. My one note of caution is not to follow every point slavishly, since such training often tries to squeeze us into a template, to be like everyone else. Media training, in particular, can make people sound professional but devoid of humanity – we're told to speak in a rather guarded way, deflecting difficult questions and switching the interview back to what we want to discuss. That might satisfy a risk-averse PR team, but it isn't going to resonate with the audience (think how irritating it is when a politician keeps reverting to a script rather than giving a straight answer to a question). It certainly wouldn't have worked for me in that crisis meeting with my colleagues: I needed to be engaging, not defensive. Learn the basics from the course: how to sit, how to dress for specific situations, how to ensure you stay on point, but always remember *what* you are trying to convey and *who* you are looking to persuade. Remember that personal-brand checklist we considered in Chapter 2? You might be representing an organisation, but similar principles apply if you want to get your message across. What are the goals? What story are you looking to tell? Consider, in any specific situation what is the *one idea* you want the audience to take away? Don't let anyone water that down.

This is especially important to note if you are just starting out in your career. It's easy to feel daunted by new situations, such as the first time you give a presentation. Most of your 'superiors' (really just colleagues who've been working longer than you) will have learned on the job, often through making mistakes and taking years to hone their presentation style, as I did. Hopefully these tips will help you feel more confident about building more character and clarity into your presentations early on, accelerating your progress.

Get a boost through training

The presentation skills training I undertook early in my career was a classroom-based course. A couple of colleagues and I were put through our paces, including being videoed and then critiqued. The concept sounds excruciating, but few people will give you honest and constructive feedback after real presentations.

They might talk about your performance afterwards, but not always to your face, and not necessarily in a way that helps you improve. The video made me squirm, but there was no hiding from reality – and what I needed to do differently. I hunched, I didn't smile enough, moved my hands awkwardly, didn't project my voice, and my clothes were wrong (too unstructured). Apart from that, all good!

The coach offered some tips. The body language checklist is obvious but often forgotten, especially in the pressure of the moment. Look people in the eye, smile warmly, stand up tall with your shoulders pinched back and down away from your ears, plant your feet firmly on the ground (that point is critical – watch out for situations where you are placed on a high stool unable to reach the ground and, if possible, ask for the set-up to be changed; it's important to feel grounded, literally). When it came to structuring a talk to convey messages effectively, he suggested that for every phase of the presentation, I make three distinct points and then remind the audience of them at the end. This seemed good advice . . . until I went along to a real-life pitch shortly afterwards. Unusually, the teams from four firms vying for the business stayed in the same room, so we heard each other's presentations. I realised we had all been on the same course (or something very similar). Everyone was making three points at the start, the middle and the end. We had blended into the same pre-senter, making it hard for any of us to stand out. With hindsight, I should have listened carefully to the advice, taken on board the specific points about body language and general need for clarity but decided for myself what I really wanted to get across – *and how*. I should have thought more about the audience's perspective; they must have been quite bored listening to four versions of the same pitch. Many years later a colleague generously praised my performance as 'host' at Newton's client conference: 'You came across so warmly,' he said afterwards. Yet in those early presentations I would have seemed quite formal and cold. I didn't bring my own personality into the room, I stuck to the conventional approach and it was far less compelling.

It's tempting (especially when we are novice presenters) to concentrate entirely on what we are saying, rather than on the audience's experience. Those talks might be intellectually sound but dull; we've all heard people speak with flawless delivery but no heart. Someone with less mastery of the subject who engages with the audience, and who puts themselves in their shoes, is far more likely to make a positive impact. As a boss, I can tell you that this is absolutely key to impressing your senior colleagues. It shows real flair and presence – qualities that are highly valued. Make a brilliant presentation to the management team and you'll be remembered for all the right reasons.

How do we do that exactly?

Patsy Rodenburg is head of voice at the Guildhall School of Music and Drama in London and the director of voice at Michael Howard Studies in New York City, and she has worked with many famous actors as well as up-and-coming talent. She declares, 'The voice encompasses so many things. Everyone comes on the planet with a fantastic voice, but people lose it. The voice is about communicating, engaging, how you show yourself, how you speak, how you listen.' She spends time on exercises for the body and breath as well as the voice. Tension in our bodies prevents our voices from being free and natural. For many years I put on a false 'special occasion' speaking voice for presentations. And my children laugh at my weird 'telephone voice'. I tend to go into a set 'phone mode', but I know that's far less effective than speaking naturally. Think of the people you enjoy listening to – radio presenters, perhaps, or chat-show hosts, as well as friends and family – you enjoy it because their voices sound relaxed and engaging. They draw you in.

Patsy has her own way of describing how we create a connection with our listeners. This is obviously critical for actors, but it's also important if any of us wants to be truly heard, including at work. Patsy describes us as operating in three different circles of energy and connectivity. The first circle is where we are inward-looking, connected more with ourselves than others, where our voice tends to fall away and we look down. The third circle is the opposite, where we might talk too loudly, exude a generalised energy that dissipates around us, over-projecting and not focusing on those we are talking to. The ideal second circle is where we are totally present, in the moment, aware, focused, with a two-way, give-and-take relationship with others. In this state, we have presence, we're not distracted by irrelevant thoughts, we are *connecting*. In that situation, people will *want* to listen to what we have to say – and we'll be interested in listening to them.

Patsy laments that we are losing our presence as a society, turning inwards, becoming more isolated, on our phones, disconnected. Sadly, this has been exacerbated by the pandemic. It's certainly harder to truly establish a genuine connection online, especially if it's our first 'meeting' with someone. Yet there is great joy to be found when we do connect. We can *learn* (or relearn), to concentrate on the other person, to consider *them* and to engage their attention – whether we are speaking online or in real life. And it's far easier to connect when we show our own humanity, that we don't have all the answers, that we are open to other ideas.

Brené Brown has written several books about the power of really connecting and emphasises that 'vulnerability is the only bridge to connection'. It makes sense: people relate to those who are honest about their doubts and imperfections. Yet it's intrinsically difficult to show vulnerability on stage or in a business context. It takes courage, for a start. It mustn't feel scripted, and oversharing isn't helpful either. If you consider a personal anecdote to be helpful to others, that's usually a good test of whether it's right to share. It's worth taking the risk. Truly connecting with our fellow human beings is rewarding in so many ways (as well as being good for our careers). Get this right and they will hear you – as well as see you, following our earlier emphasis on style – as you want to be heard and seen.

This concept of being able to connect, to inspire, is also much more appealing, modern and relevant than the old-school 'executive presence' we discussed before. The two might superficially overlap around qualities such as gravitas (being taken seriously), but the emphasis on building a genuine connection with colleagues and other audiences rather than adopting the trappings of hierarchical power is what's relevant today. The 30% Club achieved a breakthrough in its quest to see more women appointed to boards not by hectoring company chairmen but through gentle persuasion. One chairman told me that he became actively involved because 'you seemed to understand us, you were one of us'. Another went so far as to say, 'you were charming not threatening'. (I'm sure they said far less complimentary things as well.) But my approach hadn't been contrived. I really wanted chairmen to *believe* in the value of having more women on their boards and to then put their own views into practice. And once they were convinced, I certainly made it clear that I didn't have all the answers to the problem: I actively sought collaboration. Without fully appreciating it at the time, I was creating connections – and I can tell you, it works. A decade later, the percentage of women on the UK's top 350 listed boards has reached 34 per cent, up from less than 10 per cent, and there are – finally – no all-male boards (compared with over 150 when the 30% Club started).

The value of networking

The 30% Club's surprising (to me at least) success also highlights the importance of networking. There were just a handful of supporters at the start, all chairmen who I or other members of the steering committee happened to know, and in turn those chairmen drew upon their networks to create a chain reaction. I am not a natural networker – in my 20s I'd avoid business events, feeling gauche, an outsider, unsure how to start a conversation with a stranger. That made it hard to move jobs after the disappointment of being passed over for promotion – I simply didn't have the contacts or a profile within the industry. Even today, I still feel uncomfortable in certain social situations (unlike my husband, who is naturally very gregarious). If you feel the same, be selective rather than opting out. If there's someone you want to meet, try to work out what events they might be attending (easier than it sounds if they are on social media), think about what you'll say to be engaging and interesting (don't march up and ask a stranger for a favour) and make a commitment not to leave until you've introduced yourself. In other words, *strategise*. In Chapter 11 you'll hear the amazing true story of how one woman landed her dream job by doing just that. More random opportunities may arise too: I was recently stopped in a busy street by a young woman who recognised me and asked would I meet for a coffee to discuss her new job opportunity. She seized the moment and I was happy to say yes. As with everything we're discussing here, the more you practise and build your confidence, the more you'll be able to make the most of – and *create* – opportunities to connect.

Developing 'second circle' ways of communicating

Many women are naturally very good at being in the 'second circle': emotionally intelligent, empathetic, good at building a rapport. It's critical as you develop your communication style that you stay true to yourself, establishing your own brand of strong feminine power. Remember Mary Beard's exhortation to 'think about power differently'? In today's dystopian world, people increasingly want to feel a personal connection, to be inspired, to see their leader as both strong and compassionate. Different circumstances call for different leadership styles: this is a great moment for women to step forward and lead like women. At the most recent UK General Election in December 2019, a record 220 women were elected as Members of Parliament, a third of the total, helping the House of Commons better reflect the people it serves. I know and admire many of these women. They tend to dress in styles that reflect their personalities and the image they want to project in public life. But if you take a look at the House in session (you can watch it live on ParliamentTV), you'll see that the debates still tend to be characterised by hectoring, aggression and banter: at times, it's a bear pit! I'd love to see women consciously pivoting away from these masculine styles of communication. If we use our natural voices and emotional intelligence, a tipping point will be reached and the cultural norm will shift. Baroness Catherine Meyer, a colleague of mine in 'the other place' (the House of Lords), exemplifies elegance of style in both her dress and thoughtful, considerate speeches. The goal is to communicate in a way that reinforces the personal brand we are creating through our sartorial style; it doesn't make sense to dress boldly but talk timidly, wear relaxed clothes but present very formally – or dress like a woman but speak like a man.

Think of your voice and appearance as interconnected aspects of the style that reflects your substance.

Even if we are determined to act and sound like women, we might still need to work on our vocal delivery. Patsy Rodenburg recommends exercises that open up the ribcage and free the breath. It's obvious, really, but hardly the usual preparation for work presentations (including online). If it's a big occasion but you are presenting online rather than in an auditorium, as well as doing the exercises, consider standing up and resting your laptop on a windowsill so that you are not hunched over. Patsy suggests we stretch out our intercostal muscles (between the ribs) by lifting up one arm and bending to the side, repeating on the other side and then releasing our back by crossing our arms over our chests and bending over to the ground while keeping our knees soft, breathing in and out then slowly rising up. Try it: the exercises help to release tension and create better alignment in our bodies, helping us to open up and harness the power of our voice.

Find your own way to engage with the audience

The preparation above, even with good material, is obviously not enough to be a truly great speaker. Some people are naturally gifted public speakers; for the rest of us practice is key. It's very hard to come across well if you're trying to memorise a list of dos and don'ts. Over the years, I've accepted many opportunities to give talks (including some nerve-wracking ones that I really didn't look forward to) and gradually things have come more naturally. Through giving both good talks and bad, I've learned what helps me engage with the audience. This is a bit like revising for an exam: you have to learn what works for you. Reading notes is my own personal recipe for disaster – I sound wooden and contrived. And if it's an in-person talk, a lectern is a problem; it creates a physical barrier between me and the audience. If I don't need notes, it can simply be removed – and I've learned to insist on that or else just to stand in front and pace the stage while I'm speaking. If I can't learn the whole speech off by heart I have learned to keep most of it in my head by writing it out beforehand and concentrating on the way the talk flows. If I'm really worried I'll lose my place, I'll jot prompts on a page and put it in my pocket, ready if needed (obviously on those occasions I'll deliberately wear a dress or jacket with pockets). Then I practise, practise, practise, looking like a mad woman – so I do that behind closed doors although it's helpful to have a final dry run with a friendly audience, too. They can give you honest feedback. Once I was trying to master President Roosevelt's magnificent 'Man in the Arena' speech to incorporate into my own words of acceptance for an award that I'd won from the *Financial Times*; I recited it over and over, completely oblivious that someone had arrived at our house with plants for the garden. The man eventually spoke up, 'Are you an actress?' he asked. Embarrassed, I explained what I was doing. He said, encouragingly, that it sounded 'really good', and even though he was probably just being kind, that actually helped me to feel more confident (along with an emerald-green silk dress that was special yet not too overdressed for a business awards event). And, if after all this preparation, I do lose my train of thought, I've learned to pause, not panic. (I talk too quickly anyway; pauses are probably something of a relief to my audiences.) The practice eventually pays off: my maiden speech in the House of Lords during a debate on coronavirus lockdown measures would have been a terrifying prospect a decade earlier, but although I felt naturally nervous given the big occasion, *I knew I could do it* – and do it well. My confidence wasn't empty bravado, it was based on the reality of extensive preparation of the content and delivery of my short speech – including several rehearsals, without notes, in front of patient family members. As I stood up to speak I reminded myself that I deserved to be there, that the audience wanted me to succeed (maiden speeches are the one time when members of the House can count on widespread support), that I had something to contribute and that this was *a great opportunity*. I deserved to be there. You might be surprised by that claim, given that we're led to believe that the majority of women suffer from 'imposter syndrome', the feeling that we don't merit our success, that we are going to be uncovered as frauds. On this I'm with Lorraine Candy, author of *Mum, What's Wrong with You? 101 Things Only Mothers of Teenage Girls Know*. Writing in *Grazia*, Lorraine describes imposter syndrome as 'a stone in the shoe of smart women ... because even if you don't feel like an imposter you think you should because this daft phrase exists', adding that she hopes we can stamp out the expression before her two daughters aged 17 and 18 enter the workplace. It's natural to be nervous in new situations but that doesn't mean we're not capable of living up to the task. And the more airtime we give to the 'imposter' concept, the more real it becomes. Don't fall for it: you *do* deserve your success.

Think on your feet

We can't prepare for every eventuality, and learning how to adapt – how to think on our feet – is another important skill. There have been several occasions when I have walked into a room to give a presentation and found quite a different set-up from what I'd been expecting – sometimes much grander and bigger in scale. Although it's been disconcerting, I've learned to take a deep breath and to try to work out a way through. These catapulting moments can turn out to be big opportunities. A few years ago, I was asked to address a group about developments in the investment industry. I hopped in a cab and wrote a few provocations on my way over. For some reason, I thought it was a lunchtime roundtable discussion and that I was simply starting off the conversation. When I arrived, I was shown into a small-ish room set with tables as if for a meal. So far, so good. Then someone came 'to escort me to the hall' and I walked into a full auditorium (afterwards, I discovered that there were around 800 attendees). Luckily, I was first shown to a seat while the previous speaker was finishing. I glanced around (willing myself not to visibly panic), trying to gauge the dynamic, and how to develop my sparse notes. The audience seemed half asleep; I realised that the presenter was explaining a rather technical issue. Then I spotted the renowned journalist Gillian Tett seated on stage moderating the event. I suddenly saw the combination of a bigger audience and the presence of an influential commentator as an opportunity to say something really bold, to lift the room and (hopefully) galvanise the sleepy crowd. I'd long felt frustrated that the investment industry rarely spoke up about the issues of the day, that we had stood on the sidelines during the global financial crisis and that it was hardly surprising we were struggling to earn public trust and attract great young and diverse talent. I took a deep breath, collected my thoughts and started my talk by telling the audience that we needed to 'come out of the shadows'. I knew my facts and examples because this was a topic I had thought about for a long time, but I hadn't publicly articulated my views. The audience wasn't necessarily in *agreement* but they were certainly *engaged* – lots of people came up to me afterwards and wanted to discuss what I'd said. Meanwhile, Gillian Tett wrote an article for the *Financial Times* titled 'Fund managers told to come out of the shadows', helping my ideas go much further than the room. Yet five minutes before I was – literally – at a loss for words.

Of course it's much better to be prepared.

For a perfect demonstration of what to do, watch Patsy Rodenburg's videos on YouTube[21] – you'll see a woman who's the very embodiment of her 'second circle' theory: mesmerisingly good at building an emotional rapport, establishing common ground with a logical argument supported by data, facts and analysis while sharing opinions and humour. (The first comment under The Second Circle video reads 'I like how I automatically go into second circle just by listening to her.') Storytelling brings her theories alive. She is human, she is likeable, she is powerful in her own way. And Patsy speaks as if she is addressing us personally, rather than giving a speech. Most of our work interactions aren't formal presentations; they are conversations with one person or small group meetings. These are all opportunities to create a favourable impression. Presentation skills training is good practice for those everyday situations: it helps us to put ourselves in the other person's shoes and to open up, rather than cower and shrink inwards. And those everyday interactions with our colleagues and managers are in turn good practice for big moments presenting to lots of people.

Understand your body language

Asahi Pompey is president of the Goldman Sachs Foundation and the company's global head of corporate engagement. She often represents Goldman Sachs in the media, including on television and, as the most senior black woman at the firm, she is a role model for many colleagues. The number-one issue she talks about with her mentees? Opening up the body. Closed body language is a common phenomenon, especially among women. But, as Asahi notes, there's a connection between mind, body and speech: if our body is hunched, we tend to clam up. When we are relaxed, we open up verbally. The pieces all work together. And men tend to expand into their space ('man-spreading'), while women do the opposite. If you're dubious, take a look at how men and women come into the room at your next in-person meeting and see how expansive or restrictive they are as they take their seats. There will be exceptions but I'd be surprised if you don't see a pattern. If your own natural tendency is to close your body, to occupy as little space as possible, to cross your legs and perhaps slightly stoop, you need to consciously work to expand your chest, gesticulate more, reach the crown of your head to the ceiling and plant your feet firmly on the floor. Come into the room as if you are proud of who you are! If you're already confident in the way you look, you'll be better equipped to do this, but your body language needs to match.

It sounds unlikely, but one of the best demonstrations of the collective power and individual brilliance of women presenting that I've ever seen was fashion designer Edeline Lee's autumn/ winter 2019 show. London Fashion Week is a triumph of British creativity. It's also a celebration of women. But there's a catch: as Edeline points out, fashion is 'an arena where women are always seen, seldom heard'.

Her show was a magnificent response. Alongside the models wearing her beautiful collection, she invited 35 women from all walks of life to use their voices to describe how they are making an impact. I spoke about the rather unfashionable but important topic of women's finances. All the speakers were dressed in black versions of the designer's dresses, so the emphasis was on what we were saying. From 'Magic Breakfasts' for school children who don't have enough to eat in the morning at home, to exploring the critical role of women in technology, the afternoon of short talks and gorgeous dresses showcased modern feminine power. Each of the presenters spoke in their own distinctive way; their personality as well as their expertise shone through. They built on their strengths.

Switch the emphasis from weaknesses to strengths

I'm conscious that much of the advice I'm sharing might be described as self-improvement. But I'm really only encouraging you to use what you've got more effectively, not to change who you are. In fact, the trick is often to 'turn up the volume' around your strengths. Too often, the emphasis of coaching, training or advice is on fixing our weaknesses. A team of Gallup scientists, led by the late Don Clifton, described as the 'father of strengths-based psychology', found that 'people have several times more potential for growth when they invest energy in developing their strengths instead of correcting their deficiencies'.[22] This makes perfect sense to me. It is uphill work correcting our weaknesses – sometimes it has to be done, but the path to greatness is not hoed by focusing on what's wrong with us. If you concentrate instead on what's right about you and develop those strengths every single day you're far more likely to succeed.

Perhaps you're not sure what your strengths are? (Believe me, you have them.) I recommend taking the 'StrengthsFinder test'. You'll need to purchase the book *Strengthsfinder 2.0* to get an access code, but it's well worth the investment. I've taken many psychometric tests but found this the most helpful (and since it concentrates on the positives, the most enjoyable). You'll learn which are your five exceptional strengths out of 34 identified by the researchers, and you will receive a report that delves into those strengths as they apply to you specifically. I'm an 'Achiever' (a good day is one when I've achieved something), a 'Learner' (inquisitive and enjoy finding out new information), a 'Maximiser' (when I'm working with others I draw upon their strengths), and I am characterised by 'Input' (a craving to know more) and 'Belief' (my work needs to be meaningful).

Once you identify yours (either through self-awareness or taking the test), the next question is: do you have ample opportunity to use those strengths at work? The Gallup studies indicate that those who do have the opportunity to focus on their strengths every day are 'six times as likely to be engaged in their jobs and more than three times as likely to report having an excellent quality of life in general'. They are happy because they are building on what they already have rather than going against the grain.

It's important to be leveraging your strengths; it's also important to bring your personality to work. Think about the person your friends like – your engaging, true, and relaxed self. Now consider the person who presents themselves in the office or at online meetings each day. Are those two characters recognisably related? There may be facets of your relaxed self that are best left for the weekends, but you might be leaving too much of your personality at the real or virtual office door. I've worked with so many women who keep their heads down, work hard and do everything that's asked of them (including myself in that first job) but they suppress what's special. These days, special is good! As executive recruiter Upasna Bhadhal confirms, even traditional firms in male-dominated sectors now want 'to be connected with diverse talent'. They are looking for diversity of thought, creative and innovative ideas, a spark. Their promotion and reward systems might be lagging, but senior executives know they don't have a connection with the next generation of customers, or a good understanding about how the future will unfold, only that it is likely to be very different from the past. They are ready to listen. Speak up, be heard, be inventive. You don't need to be an extrovert; you just need to meet their gaze, be prepared for those opportunities to speak up and say what you have to say in your own way. Whatever the context, people love stories, real-life anecdotes that bring your ideas to life. Show your emotional intelligence by relating to your audience and offering solutions, not problems.

Your bosses will love that.

Takeaways from Chapter 4

1. Displaying grace under fire works far better than 'losing it' in difficult moments – however challenging that may feel.

2. Use social media to build your brand and a network. Use to your advantage the knowledge that employers will do a sweep of your social-media presence: create a profile that's interesting and thoughtful.

3. Presentation skills training can be useful but also generic. Use it to learn how to hold your body, and how to project but ensure your messages remain true and not 'manu-factured'. Decide what are the key points you want the audience to hear and the best – most engaging – means of conveying them. Don't stick to a formula, be yourself.

4. Connecting with your audience is key to a great presenta-tion. Put yourself in the audience's position and consider their perspective. Create emotional engagement. A talk with heart and a few fluffed lines is far better than a word-perfect wooden presentation.

→

5. Everyday opportunities, such as presentations to colleagues, are chances to practise for the bigger stage.

6. Learn what works for you. Notes, no notes? Slides, no slides? Humour? Quotes? Believe in yourself and what you are saying. Practise, practise, practise! Don't panic if the situation is different from what you've been led to expect. Deep breath. Focus on what you know.

7. Open up your body. Stretch your intercostal muscles beforehand. Walk proudly into the room wearing an outfit that boosts your confidence. Plant your feet firmly on the ground. Look into the audience's eyes before you begin. Connect as human beings.

8. Aim for your style of communication and appearance to align. (One might lead the other as you build your confidence.) If you dress like a woman, make sure you sound like one too: use your natural voice, powers of persuasion and emotional intelligence.

9. Build on your strengths. Focus on what's right about you. Identify those strengths and then maximise the opportunities to demonstrate and build on them.

10. Bring your personality to work. Difference is welcomed. Speak up when you have an idea. Build your confidence and the confidence of those around you by actively participating. Focus on offering solutions wherever possible.

Chapter 5

How to be 'Put-together': Mastering Hair and Make-Up for Work

'There's more to make-up than meets the eye.'

The Renfrew Center Foundation

We've now covered the basics for confident style when it comes to both workwear and communication. But what about that other potential minefield, often described as 'grooming': hair and make-up? Far from being frivolous, mastering these aspects of our appearance can boost our mental health as well as our image and career prospects. Hair and make-up make a particular impact online, when just our head and shoulders are on view. And yet, once again, this is a subject that is rarely broached for career women, leaving us trying to decipher the beauty codes for ourselves, perhaps never quite sure whether we've got it right. The redoubtable broadcaster Emma Barnett took me to task on her BBC Radio 5 *Live* show: was I suggesting that 'women should discuss pink lipstick in the office' and risk not being taken seriously? No – although arguably it shouldn't matter – men spend a *lot* of time talking about 'last night's game'. As Goldman's Asahi Pompey says in the context of her high-powered role in finance, 'We can talk about lipstick *and* capital markets. No one thinks if men talk about sport they can't talk about the markets.' Whatever your views about what we should discuss at work, if wearing the right make-up helps women feel good about ourselves *and* helps us to be seen as capable, we should be getting (and giving) all the advice we need.

Wearing make-up is not about 'succumbing to the patriarchy' (unless the only reason you're wearing make-up is to please men). It's about using what's available to help us to feel more confident – which will in turn help us to succeed. As we've firmly established, appearances count. In Chapter 1 we learned that it takes just a tenth of a second for someone to form an opinion of a stranger from their face alone. Research conducted by Harvard Medical School and Massachusetts General Hospital suggests that people take a mere quarter of a second to assess our competence, likeability and trustworthiness.[23] And we're *hard-wired* to rate those who look 'put-together' higher than those who don't, irrespective of what else we learn about them. Psychologist Linda Albright conducted a fascinating experiment. She and her colleagues at Westfield State University in America wondered, 'If individuals were asked to make judgements about the personality characteristics of people they had never met, based on photographs alone, how much *consensus* would there be? With no behavioural evidence to go on, we might intuitively expect there to be little or zero consensus.' But in reality, we take clues from people's appearance that fit our shared stereotypes – to a surprising degree. Professor Albright and her colleagues found that 'type of clothing, hairstyle and personal grooming all convey information about people's conscientiousness'.[24] If we *look* physically put-together, people assume that we are mentally put-together, too – and they make inferences about our capability, our competency and our conscientiousness. That's quite a leap from a photo. The good news is that we can *do something* about how polished we are.

The benefits of wearing make-up

A more difficult challenge might be dealing with the 'beauty bias' that's been shown to exist in the labour market. A comprehensive academic study pulling together perspectives from economics, social psychology and evolutionary psychology concluded, 'Physically attractive individuals are more likely to be interviewed for jobs and hired, they are more likely to advance rapidly in their careers through frequent promotions and they earn higher wages than unattractive individuals.'[25] Good-looking people do have some things easier in life, but many people succeed, across the full spectrum of attractiveness (a very subjective measure in any case). In any event, good make-up can enhance what we've got – and it turns out, it might have more of a bearing on how 'attractive' we are considered to be. A young banker friend, who's very beautiful, told me she'd read that women who wear make-up at work get paid an extra 20 per cent. I hadn't heard that and thought it seemed quite an extreme 'beauty bonus'. It turns out that a study by sociologists Jaclyn Wong and Andrew Penner, based on data collected from over 14,000 employees, confirms that there is a link between income and 'effort-based' attractiveness – especially for women – and that the differential is indeed as much as 20 per cent.[26] We might be annoyed about being judged in this way, but we do have control over the effort we make over our appearance.

We can also gain emotional and psychological benefits from

wearing make-up. There are competing hypotheses: *either* women wear make-up because we have low self-esteem and are trying to camouflage flaws/hide behind a mask *or* we wear make-up to enhance our looks and to control how we are perceived. The former sparks criticism of the beauty industry for making us feel inadequate, the latter seems empowering.

Both explanations can apply, depending on how we are feeling at a particular moment in our lives. Of course, there are some women who really do look better without make-up – my daughter Florence has always been a fresh-faced beauty with great bone structure, full lips and bright turquoise-blue eyes. Just a moderate amount of make-up seems to diminish rather than enhance her looks, so even her wedding day make-up was barely noticeable. (And it wasn't one of those laborious 'no make-up' make-up looks that really involves many products and considerable time.) At the other end of the spectrum, some women feel that they need to be fully made-up to present themselves even to their own families. Others are reasonably comfortable in their own skin and use make-up depending on the situation.

Whatever our natural starting point, *we tend to feel better when we think we look better.* Personally, I feel naked without make-up, and if I am wearing none (or very little) people ask after my health. (This would have been just as true in my thirties or forties as it is today.) Comments like 'Are you OK? You look rather tired' make me *feel* exhausted. Make-up can conceal those under-eye shadows, give a little healthy glow to our cheeks and open up tired eyes. For many of us, it can put a spring in our step.

As with other aspects of our appearance, there's scope for beauty blunders. The scene in the movie *Bridget Jones* when the heroine slathers on too much blusher in the back of a taxi en route to a big gala dinner is literally a slapstick version of a mistake many of us have made. Good lighting is essential (stand next to a window if your bathroom light doesn't suffice) and a few other basic principles can help when it comes to choosing and applying the right make-up for work – including asking a friend or colleague for their opinion. We have got ourselves into a situation where we might feel embarrassed to ask, especially in a work context, but that reluctance means that we're not helping each other out as much as we could – and would be happy to. The reality is that well-applied, subtle but confident make-up can give you a head start in the perception stakes. In one of their research studies, Sylvia Ann Hewlett and her team at the Center for Talent Innovation asked people (both men and women) to assess women's make-up in terms of suitability for work. They made up the same woman to varying degrees, starting *au naturel* and ending with a heavy, full face of make-up including eyelash extensions. Interestingly, both men and women agreed that the third option, properly made-up but not as intense as the fourth look, was best, but the main finding was most reassuring: as long as a woman looked groomed and had taken care with her make-up and hair, using sophisticated colours (read nothing too bright or obvious) and blending well, the reaction was positive. Respect and credibility are ours to win or lose – well-applied make-up gets us off to a good start.

Building on a good foundation

It turns out that the make-up product that has the biggest impact on how others assess our professionalism is foundation. It evens out skin tone and creates a polished base. I have erred through much of my career: I have pale freckly skin and, up until quite recently, felt that foundation hid those freckles that are part of me and my personality. Don't get me wrong, I am not a big fan of those freckles (as a young girl I used to try to remove them with lemon juice, which really doesn't work), but I thought that foundation 'blanked' me out and made me look even paler. I started to realise, however, that I was missing a trick. Whenever I did TV interviews or magazine shoots, the make-up artist always spent most of her time on the 'base'. I saw that even a light foundation (one that lets my freckles peek through) is the starting point for a polished look, and without it other products tended to sit a bit starkly on my face, not blending well. I have learned to use those ad hoc make-up sessions ahead of TV appearances or photo shoots to ask lots of questions. Make-up artists have usually spent considerable time and effort researching the best products and are generally happy to share their advice. I take pictures on my phone, so that I can recall their recommendations. These tutorials have since been very useful for Zoom as well as remote TV appearances.

I've also watched some great online lessons that are geared towards career rather than glamour make-up. Trinny Woodall's short YouTube videos (my favourite is 'How to Wake Up a Washed-Out Face') are short, honest and fun. She uses her own Trinny London make-up and skincare range, but her advice works with similar products from other brands. I'm a fan of Charlotte Tilbury make-up, partly because her Magic moisturiser really does seem to work like magic on my dry skin, but as with all the other aspects of your appearance, the key is to experiment until you find what works best for you. There are now good 'ethical beauty' products available, brands such as PHB Ethical Beauty, and www.sustainablejungle.com offers a helpful itemised rating of leading brands. It's also worth investing in decent brushes; fingertips are great for applying and blending certain products (eye shadow, for example) but a big soft brush for bronzer and blusher is essential, and I also rely on a thin slanted brush for filling in my sparse eyebrows and softening eyeliner.

Make-up artists' tips

Your best colours will obviously depend on your skin tone, eye colour and desired strength of look, but the make-up artists' basic steps and products are always the same. On the basis of their advice, here's what's in my make-up bag and how I apply everything for my everyday 'work face'. The whole routine takes ten minutes.

A great moisturiser, plus time to prepare the skin. Net-a-Porter asked me to do a photo shoot to celebrate the company's 20-year anniversary. It was during the first wave of the pandemic and no one was allowed on set apart from the photographer, so I was treated to an online 'glamour session'. The beautician showed me how to create a more glowing complexion by massaging my face with moisturiser, taking a few minutes to apply it with small circular movements starting at the neck and working up to the forehead and temples, sweeping out and concentrating a little more around the eyes and jawline. It really gives a dewy finish that lasts better than a perfunctory application, especially when I leave it for a few moments before applying foundation. (I use that time to apply body moisturiser.)

A lightweight foundation which I dot all over my face and blend (but don't rub) in before checking the jawline and hairline for tidemarks.

Concealer I've experimented for years to find one that gives good coverage but doesn't cake – my favourite is Magic Away by Charlotte Tilbury, helpfully labelled in shades to match the brand's foundation. I apply this liberally to all the red areas (often round the nose), dark circles under my eyes and other blemishes

(I have greenish veins around the temples – lovely!) – and blend so that it's even.

Eyebrow shadow in mid brown (I prefer this to a pencil, as it looks more natural). I use Bourjois eyebrow palette, which includes a colour that gives definition without making my brows unnaturally dark. I use that slanted brush to apply the shadow gradually to my brows, working from the section closest to my nose, sweeping from below then moving up and over the brow through the arch (my brows aren't really arched, so I create an illusion with this under–over technique).

Bronzer I use the fabulous 'Ambient' bronzer palette by Hourglass. It contains three soft, slightly shimmering colours. I swish a big fat brush over all three and apply to my cheeks and then use what remains on the brush for my jawline and around my hairline to give a little extra definition and colour. This looks quite natural on my skin colour – you might prefer to use blusher.

Eye shadows I like a light gold on my lids, then a soft coppery brown in the eye socket. It's tricky to find all the best colours in one palette, so I take my favourites from a couple including an inexpensive Maybelline set, which includes lovely coppery shades and a darker one for smudging eyeliner. The key to finding the right make-up shades is establishing whether your skin has cool or warm undertones. Mine are warm although when a make-up artist first used these gold and coppery colours on my eyes I thought they might make me look tired. With good blending and completing the eye with liner and mascara, I can see the overall effect is more flattering than cooler shades, which look ashen on my skin. The whites of my eyes also look brighter. (I often wear contact lenses and suffer from dry eyes, so anything that can help diminish redness is welcome.)

Eye pencil I love 'Classic Brown' by Charlotte Tilbury (previously called 'Audrey'). I draw a fine line close to my eyelashes top and bottom, avoiding the inner corners of the eyes, as that would make my eyes look closer-set.

A dark eye shadow to soften the eyeliner, taken from the Maybelline palette mentioned above. I then smudge the line and thicken it a little towards the outer edges of my eyes to help my eyes look more defined and vaguely almond-shaped. I use that slanted brush again, taking care to shake any excess eye shadow off the brush before starting around my eyes.

Black mascara I have pathetic eyelashes. I have found two mascaras that really work: Dior's Diorshow and Charlotte Tilbury's Pillow Talk Push Up Lashes. Neither are cheap, so when able to travel I stock up on the more expensive make-up brands at airports.

Blusher At this stage, when everything is almost finished I apply a little pinkish blusher to the apples of my cheeks, perhaps also a little to the area under my brow and around my temples. I leave this to the end to gauge if it's necessary. Some days we look tired, other days refreshed – a pop of pink just gives me some extra help if needed. I have an Estée Lauder blusher palette that, again, has a few shades and again I swirl that big brush over to create a blend. It's tricky to find a single colour that works – a palette lets us create something more closely approximating the multiple colours in our natural skin.

Powder I use translucent powder to take any shine off my fore-head and chin and to set the concealer under my eyes. I don't apply to other parts of my face, as it makes everything seem too layered and dull. Charlotte Tilbury's is a very fine almost-invisible powder; No 7 makes a good one too.

Lipstick Shade, density and amount of gloss is obviously a matter of personal preference. For work, I like a nude shade that just deepens my natural lip colour. Charlotte Tilbury's Pillow Talk in its original form is a perfect shade for a natural look.

I always do my make-up first thing in the morning after my shower, let it settle then take another quick look (in broad daylight) before leaving for the office or joining my first Zoom meeting – it usually needs a second go-over at that point. I keep a small cosmetic bag with essentials in my handbag or on my home-working desk for quick touch-ups during the day.

These are the basic steps and product checklist (to be adapted to your own colouring, of course) for the simplest fail-safe polished make-up look, although you might prefer something a little more distinctive. Suman Sidhu, who always looks immaculate, told me that she used to wear stronger make-up than her colleagues – including eyelash extensions and lip liner. She began to feel unsure that she wanted to stand out for her make-up, and has since dialled it down and is happier with a more natural, yet still carefully applied look. If you work in a creative field, there's more scope for experimentation than in a corporate setting, although I know one or two very successful female bankers who wear serious dark clothes with a dash of red lipstick: a great combination. Goldman's Asahi Pompey loves Fenty Beauty's 'Stunna Lip Paint' in 'Uncensored' – a true red. There are also international differences. When appearing on television in America, I've been put through a sort of TV-anchor-woman-machine, emerging with big hair and glossy lips – much to my husband's amusement. Last time I was on American TV he texted me afterwards, 'Didn't they have a mirror?' They did, but by the time I glanced up at my reflection, it was too late to do much about the scary apparition looking back. Since then I've kept an eye on how the hair and make-up is progressing. In reality, just as with clothes, the point is not to create carbon-copy looks, we're looking to enhance what we have, to look on top of our game. We know we can be trusted with highly complex tasks and problems – the right make-up ensures that others see us that way as well, even at our first meeting.

Good hair days

Hair is another potentially tricky area, especially given the wide range of hair types we are blessed with (or perhaps rather less than blessed – my hair is very average, even on a good day). Our relationship with our hair is complex. Over centuries, women's hair has been associated with femininity, attractiveness, freedom and identity. That's a lot of pressure on hair! If our hair is very fine, frizzy, dry, greasy or, worst of all, falling out, it can seriously affect our self-esteem. And even women with great hair can equate a bad hair day with a bad day, full stop.

I've had many struggles with my hair over the years, suffering several episodes of quite severe hair loss after stressful times or after I've stopped breastfeeding. Stress is often a causal factor; it's thought that the physical and emotional stress of having COVID-19 might explain why some sufferers experience hair loss months after recovering from the virus. The problem is that the added stress of losing our hair makes it hard to break the cycle.

My way of coping is to take supplements. Even if it's too late to stop the shedding (there's a three-month lag), it helps to reassure me that the problem won't continue. And I've tended to wear my hair up to disguise its wispiness during those times. A great friend remarked that she liked my hair up, and I confessed that it was to hide the problem. She told me (and I believed her) that she hadn't noticed, thanks to the up-do. Eventually, my hair grew back and I could wear it loose again. If you have a major hair concern that isn't related to something obvious like chemotherapy, I recommend seeing a trichologist, who will test for any mineral or vitamin deficiencies or hormonal imbalances that might be the cause (and might be undermining your general health as well). Hormones are quite often to blame: Jenny Halpern Prince was 'incredulous' that she still had any hair left after losing so much during the perimenopause (and as you'll hear later, Jenny's beautiful long blonde hair is a big part of her look). She now takes supplements from Victoria Health. It's not worth suffering in silence or assuming nothing can be done. (But remember, even the professionals sometimes get it wrong. If a specialist gives you a gloomy prognosis do seek another opinion – there are cases of young women being told their hair won't ever grow again, only for that to be untrue.)

Even when my hair's been healthy, the photographic evidence shows that I've worn my hair too long, too short, too dark and too light at different times. I ultimately found my 'hair mojo' by sticking with the same salon – Nyumba, just off London's Sloane Square – for many years and trusting the colourist and stylist to decide what suits me. They know my work is serious and by developing an understanding of my life and career alongside the shape of my face and the limitations of my hair, they have come up with a style and colour that works *and* is relatively low maintenance. Every now and again we chat about whether the colour needs deepening or lightening, whether the cut should be shorter or shaped slightly differently, and I know that these conversations will reflect their honest observations about how my appearance is changing. It's great to be able to leave it to the experts – and every time they suggest a change, I can see afterwards that it was just what was needed. It took me a while to find the right hairdresser. If you're not entirely happy with yours (I used to feel a bit uncomfortable going to the previous salon – a clue that it wasn't right for me), just try somewhere else. It's not you – it's just not a good fit.

Hair and our image

If you haven't seen the 1980's classic *Working Girl* starring Melanie Griffith, Harrison Ford and Sigourney Weaver, do watch it – the film's a bit dated, but it explores the link between image and career potential very well. Melanie Griffith's character, Tess McGill, is a stockbroker's secretary who takes evening classes for a bachelor's degree in business studies. She's desperate to be elevated from her lowly job and is always coming up with good merger and acquisition ideas. At the start of the movie, Tess's long bright frizzy hair distracts us, along with her jangly jewellery. No one takes her seriously – worse, they sexually harass and humiliate her. As she seeks to emulate Sigourney Weaver's executive style, her friend cuts her frizzy hair into a sleek bob, she sheds the jewellery, mimics her boss's sophisticated elocution and borrows her clothes (one of the best lines in the movie, when Tess reads the price tag hanging on a dress in her boss's closet: 'Six thousand dollars. Six THOUSAND dollars. *And it's not even leather!*'). It's all quite obvious stuff, but her transformation is both physical and psychological. Tess McGill grows in confidence along with her polish, and suddenly everyone is assuming that she is one of the 'players': an investment banker rather than a junior assistant.

At this point, you might be thinking: *But doesn't that show how ridiculous the whole thing is?* Tess McGill is the same person throughout, yet a haircut and elegant clothes suddenly open doors – along with her own bravado. As we obtain more positions of power, as women of all shapes, colours, sizes and ages wield influence, run businesses and gain authority, we can set the rules and show the world the benefits of true diversity – including how we choose to wear our hair. As my own career has developed, my inner strength has also grown, and I've felt I have more latitude around my appearance. Being more authentic has in turn reinforced my inner strength. Getting on to that virtuous circle is the aim, and even then there will be certain situations where it's best not to push the boundaries too far. At Newton, we held an annual seminar for institutional clients. It was an event that required a lot of planning, much rehearsal and the careful orchestration of topics, presenters and the flow of the day. Every year I was interested to see how my colleagues dressed. We all were better versions of our daily selves, both men and women wearing their sharpest suits and dresses, often a little stronger in colour and cleaner in cut than for every day, with the women having spent more time on their hair and make-up than usual. 'Ourselves', just smarter, more polished and more confident. Our appearances created a backdrop for our voices: we were there to be heard, not just seen, but everyone made an effort to *look* commanding.

'Unconventional' hair

Some people have natural advantages when it comes to their appearance. As we've seen, height is a valuable attribute. It can also feel as if we have natural *disadvantages* – including 'unconventional' hair. A friend of mine – who's white – has extraordinarily curly hair, beautiful worn loose but hardly ever allowed to escape from a tight up-do in the office. My friend explains that she just feels less 'owned' by her hair if it's tucked out of sight. That seems fine since it's her choice, but if you Google 'hair discrimination' or 'hair oppression', you'll find a litany of stories about black women (and schoolchildren) being excluded or penalised for their afro-textured hair. In July 2019, California became the first state in the United States to ban the racial discrimination of natural hair in the workplace, adopting the CROWN Act (Creating a Respectful and Open World for Natural Hair), followed soon after by New York. But there are still 37 states where employers and schools can discriminate on the basis of hair. In September 2020, *Glamour* magazine, a US publication, featured six black women on the cover who all described being targeted at work, and in some cases lost their jobs, when they refused to change their natural looks. One, Brittany Noble, a newscaster, explained how costly it was to maintain her 'anchor bob' (sew-in wigs cost between $700 and $800 and the alternative of straightening her own hair every day was causing damage), so she decided to embrace her natural hair on camera. In 2018, she was fired from the news station she worked at in Mississippi (which has still to adopt the CROWN Act) having been told that her hair looked 'unprofessional'. Brittany filed a case with the US Equal Employment Opportunity Commission who investigated and gave her permission to file with the Federal Court, where her case is ongoing at the time of writing. As Brittany said to students at Penn State University, 'For me as the morning anchor, I'm thinking, if you can't get past my looks, no wonder you're not telling the stories about my community, if you can't get past my looks, no wonder we don't have more people that look like me on TV, if you can't get past my looks, no wonder we're coming into these problems . . . for me it's so much bigger [than my hair].'

In the UK, hair is not specifically mentioned in the Equality Act 2010, and although an employer can't discriminate on the basis of race, a 2020 survey undertaken by the Halo Collective found that one in five black women felt pressured to straighten their hair to look 'professional' for work – in other words to make their hair more like the average white woman's. This is shocking, yet it sadly rings true. 'Professionalism' is too often viewed through the narrow purview of Caucasian looks. At the same time, we are widely encouraged to be authentic, to 'bring ourselves' to work. And we can all accept certain boundaries. Extreme hairstyles might suggest a lack of respect for or awareness of our environment. Anything that is *deliberately provocative* creates a hurdle. But wearing black hair in all its natural beauty? How could that be an issue?

Asahi Pompey wore dreadlocks for the first 15 years of her career, right up to being promoted to managing director at Goldman Sachs. I've seen pictures that prove it – Asahi looks beautiful and immaculate, with very long dreadlocks. Women would come up to her and say, 'Wow, how amazing, I feel I can now wear my natural hair', but she was also told, 'you can't make managing director with hair like that'. Having proved the doubters wrong, Asahi felt she wanted to make a change, but given her accidental status as a natural-hair role model, she found it a 'hand-wringing' experience. Nowadays, she happily wears her hair long, sleek and straight – just because she wants to.

I first met innovation consultant Kristy McKenzie when we were both interviewed for a podcast comparing different generations' attitudes to money, savings and investments. Kristy was then 27. She is incredibly articulate and very stylish: she had piled her hair on top of her head in a dramatic bun. The next time we met she was wearing her hair curly and loose. She explained that as a child she was the only one with natural hair among her black friends. They chose to wear weaves or to chemically straighten their hair. Kristy's mum encouraged her and her younger sisters to believe that their natural hair was beautiful. Nowadays, Kristy says that she varies her hair looks partly to protect her hair, braiding and plaiting when it needs extra care and letting it loose when she's happy with its condition. It's her choice.

Every woman and girl should have the right to choose. The Halo Collective has created the Halo Code* for both schools and employers to protect anyone who comes to school or to work with natural hair and protective hairstyles associated with their racial, ethnic and cultural identities. The first employer to adopt and sign the code was Unilever, maker of Dove soap, which said, 'We know it's really important for people to be able to be themselves in the workplace.' It's a statement that the company echoes in its famous adverts for Dove, celebrating 'real women' – all beautiful in their own way.

Let's give the final word on this subject to Mellody Hobson, who I mentioned in the opening chapter. (If you want to read more, however, I highly recommend *Don't Touch my Hair* by Emma Dabiri.) When I first met Mellody I was struck by her flattering pixie cut. The effect was chic, gamine – and very distinct. Mellody is a role model for many women in business, whether they are black, white or any colour in between. In a McKinsey podcast, Mellody recounted how she decided to work *with* her difference, finding herself the only black woman at almost every meeting. 'When I started working in business, I decided to use those things to my advantage. When I go into rooms, I'm unusual. Instead of being demure about it, understand that you're going to

* The Halo Code is a campaign pledge signed by schools and businesses that promises members of the Black community that they have the 'freedom and security to wear all afro-hairstyles without restriction or judgment'. This includes any child at school.

stand out. I would go to investment conferences and Wall Street things, and people come up to me and say, "Oh, you're Mellody." I'm, like, "How do they know that?" Well, it's because I was the only one. Then I started to say, like, "I could be like Beyoncé or Cher. I don't even need Hobson." I'm going to milk this, the standing out. I'm going to make it work for me as opposed to make it some cross that I'm bearing. And the times in which people are not open or receptive to that aspect of me, I'm going to figure out how to be unapologetic about who I am.'

It's a liberating, exhilarating approach. That tactic, along with Mellody's fabled work ethic, has paid off, with her appointment as the first black chairwoman of a Fortune 500 company and so many other achievements, including raising hundreds of millions of dollars for an endeavour called Project Black, to invest in sustainable minority-owned businesses.

Be unapologetic about who you are. Work your difference. It's the same advice I gave to a mentee, looking ahead to her next role. She's had a successful 20-year career in finance and she also happens to be black. That's a rare and sought-after demographic as companies seek diverse talent at leadership levels. Would she mind being shown opportunities *because* she is a senior black woman in finance? Absolutely not! Once she gets the job, she can show them that she's brilliant. The important thing is having the opportunity to demonstrate that. I believe we're more likely today to have those chances if we make our differences work for us – and if we look like we are ready for any challenge. I mentioned in Chapter 1 that I know many brilliant and successful women: they are diverse but similar in all being comfortable in their own skin. It becomes hard to work out which came first: their self-assurance or their success, their style or their substance. Everything seems interconnected.

As these women have made progress in their achievements they've become more confident, which has spurred them on to yet greater things – and enhanced that sense that they are fundamentally happy with themselves. Lovely hair and beautifully applied make-up won't get us there, of course, but they can help us to *feel* confident that we are presenting ourselves in the best possible light, able to focus on the tasks ahead. As the advertisement for Aussie shampoo suggests, 'There's more to life than hair, but it's a good place to start!'

Having covered the (literal) foundations of your look, let's consider those finishing touches that can make or break an outfit: accessories.

Takeaways from Chapter 5

1. It's easier to concentrate on matters of substance if we feel good about ourselves. Good hair and make-up can help us feel positive, project confidence and be seen as polished and put-together. It makes sense to think about how we use these aspects of our appearance to best effect at work.

2. The evidence suggests that we don't 'need' to be beautiful (thank goodness), we just need to look groomed – that we've made an effort.

3. The most important thing about your hairstyle for work is that it makes you feel good. (But think carefully about extreme looks or hair colours – you can hopefully be authentic without being deliberately provocative.) Try to find a hairdresser who you can trust and can advise you if needed, especially when you are going through any life or career change.

→

4. Getting make-up right can boost your self-esteem. Invest time and energy to work out the right products and make-up routine for you. It needn't take long to get ready in the morning once you are confident that you have worked this out.

5. If you experience unexplained hair loss or problematic skin conditions, seek help. Stress is often a factor (and we'll consider how to manage your time and health in Chapter 8) but you might have a deficiency or hormone imbalance that can be treated. Feeling hopeful about a solution can help to break the stress cycle.

6. 'Professionalism' is too often viewed through the narrow purview of Caucasian looks. We all have a role to play to change this. Watch out for other women – if you hear someone criticised for 'unprofessional' hair when it's a natural look, speak up.

7. Be unapologetic about who you are. Work your differences. If you can combine expertise, experience and aptitude with authenticity, you're on the path to greatness.

Chapter 6

The Art of Accessorising: Shoes, Handbags, Glasses, Jewellery and Scarves – the Finishing Touches

'Put your money into accessories. You could create a million different looks.'

Iris Apfel, businesswoman, interior designer and fashion icon

Accessories are a wonderful way to pull an outfit together: a great bag, scarf, necklace or pair of shoes provides both the finishing touch and a subtle way of expressing our individuality. As Iris Apfel, born in 1921 and an undisputed style queen, points out, they can enable us to create multiple looks from a small wardrobe. And we don't need to be a certain dress size or body shape to wear beautiful accessories – perhaps this is one reason why we might keep buying lovely shoes that we don't really need. Working from home has shifted attention away from our feet to our head, neck and shoulders: a beautiful necklace or gorgeous silk scarf can transform a woolly jumper or plain T-shirt into something appropriate for a Zoom meeting while our favourite handbags and high heels gather dust. With the increasing adoption of hybrid working, we're going to cover both what works for the physical office and when you're working from home.

Shoes and confidence

Shoes are not just an easy way to express ourselves, they can enhance the rest of our outfit – and even our confidence levels. British advertising executive Beth Salmen says that having emerged from university with a first-class masters degree and feeling confident in both her abilities and style, she soon felt a little out of her depth. After a short stint as an assistant, Beth was quickly promoted to a role that involved meeting and negotiating with senior executives from luxury brands – brands that were well out of her price range. She started putting a lot of thought into her outfits, feeling that she needed to do that to 'have the right to be there'. Beth started each look with her shoes, investing in classic smart pairs with heels and making sure that they were always clean and polished. This made her feel that she had presence – that she could hold her own. (Of course, she could do that based on her ability; the heels bestowed the confidence she lacked.) Literally putting her best foot forward, Beth then built up her daily look with a sure touch, mixing tailored and relaxed pieces, playing with textures, and combining, say, a pencil skirt made out of shiny fabric with a distressed leather jacket. Beth then injured her foot quite badly and wasn't able to wear heels for a while. Forced to wear trainers or flats she 'felt a bit lost'. Much of Beth's sense of loss was down to her self-image: she was so used to her look starting with smart heels that she felt less able to make an impact in trainers.

I felt the same way when a foot operation forced me to wear a hideous surgical boot for several weeks and then my husband's trainers for months after that because my own shoes didn't fit. It might sound crazy, but my self-esteem collapsed. And yet Beth and I agree that lots of *other* women look great in trainers. I've got to know Stella McCartney over the past few years through mutual interests. She is the perfect athletic model for her own, ultra-cool, streamlined designs, including vegan bags and shoes. Often, she's dashing past me (we live close to each other), bringing one of her children to school, rushing to get to her office (also local) or on a run. Every time, she looks effortlessly amazing and instantly recognisable even before I've seen her face. And usually she's wearing practical and cool trainers, even with quite formal clothes.

Why, then, can't Beth and I believe that we might also be able to pull off such a look? I offer two explanations. The first is that we've learned what works for us at work, as far as style goes. It's taken us some time (much longer in my case) but we finally feel confident in our workwear – including smart, classic shoes. But we haven't really had the same practice or given it so much thought when it comes to more casual looks, and we certainly don't have the confidence to mix things up. Others are 'naturals' when it comes to knowing what to wear in any situation; they happily switch gears according to the occasion and look just as great in their casual clothes and unexpected combinations as they do in more formal gear. My husband is 100 per cent sure that this explanation is why I'm a bit geeky when it comes to weekend wear. The solution? To focus more on this area of my wardrobe so that I develop a similar level of confidence about it, especially now that I'm often working from home.

Another explanation is that it's easy to get stuck in a style rut. Having a consistent strong personal brand doesn't preclude experimentation – or evolution. Once we've found a style that works, it's important not to let that become a straitjacket. As our life and goals progress, our style should move on too – including our footwear.

The right shoes for getting your foot on the ladder

A top business school invited me to speak to a select group of senior women working in the charitable sector. They were all CEOs of major charities, interested in becoming non-executive directors on corporate boards. They were attending a course to help them prepare for such a role. The syllabus looked excellent. I spoke alongside advisers from a leading executive search firm, well known for its commercial board practice work. Our collective emphasis was on how these women could make the transition from 'not-for-profit' to 'for-profit' roles. We discussed how to position a CV to highlight commercial experience, to convey business acumen in interviews and to talk about financial management skills. As one of the advisers said, the risk was that these candidates' not-for-profit expertise would be seen as *anti*-profit.

Eighteen months later, none of the women had been appointed to a corporate board. I was initially surprised. They were all highly capable, several were very well known for their achievements, and they had led organisations that were complex and sizeable. They were also committed to the goal of becoming company directors. What had gone wrong? Then I recollected a thought that had fleetingly crossed through my mind during the session I attended. It sounds clichéd, but several of the women were wearing flat brown open-toed sandals. I remembered thinking that someone needed to advise them about shoes; the corporate world expected corporate shoes. I should have been that person, but I'm ashamed to say that I felt embarrassed about raising the topic. I'm now sure that no one ever did.

Women are ridiculed for the 'obsession' some of us have with shoes. A shoe habit isn't a good thing – but it's usually relatively harmless. I have several pairs of beautiful evening shoes that give me great pleasure, even if they don't get a lot of use. They are a joy to behold! Luckily four of my daughters are the same shoe size, so I can also justify the spend on the basis that we can all share. Whether you have one pair of 'good' shoes or 50, shoes can reveal quite a lot. I have been fortunate to receive several honorary doctorates. This usually involves being added on to a graduation ceremony and giving a speech. The honouree sits on the stage while each graduate comes up to receive their degree from the university chancellor, cloaked in their academic robe and mortar board – with their shoes just about the only clue as to their personality. Since there might be literally hundreds of graduates and the ceremony may take several hours, shoe watching becomes quite a fun part of it. I have seen *everything*. The highest most sparkly heels that can hardly be walked in, to dirty trainers. And yes, I do make an instant assessment of each person, even though I know they are so much more than their shoes! What do your shoes tell other people about you?

High heels – sexist or empowering?

I'm often asked if I think that high heels are sexist. It's not a straightforward question. As with make-up, if wearing heels makes us feel more confident, then no. I like the extra height and that they make me stand up straight and walk more deliberately. It's just a personal preference for situations where I need to feel authoritative. My young and beautiful banker friend, the only woman in her team, is tall and feels awkward towering over her male colleagues. Birgit Neu, who's even taller, is totally comfortable in very high heels. Suman Sidhu, five feet eight, is happier in flats – and notes that other women in her office also tend to wear flat shoes; perhaps they've influenced each other. We are all making a choice. But if you are forced to wear heels even when you find them uncomfortable, that is problematic. In 2016, temporary receptionist Nicola Thorp arrived at accountancy firm PwC in flat shoes and was told that she had to wear shoes with a heel of between 2 and 4 inches (5 and 10cm). (This was not actually PwC's policy but the outsourcing firm's.) Sent home without pay, Ms Thorp started an online petition to make it illegal for employers to require staff to wear high heels, garnering over 150,000 signatures and triggering a parliamentary debate. MPs on the Petitions Committee decided to investigate the issue with the Women and Equalities Committee. They published a joint report on high heels and workplace dress codes. The report concluded that the Equality Act 2010 *isn't* fully effective in protecting workers from discrimination around what they are required to wear. It seemed a wonderful David versus Goliath moment, but ultimately the Government ruled out a change in the law. Employers can continue to insist that female employees wear high heels if they can justify it as a requirement of the role and if men are expected to dress to an 'equivalent level of smartness' (although clearly this is unlikely to require wearing uncomfortable shoes). The Government Equalities Office later (May 2018) published new guidelines around dress codes at work to help both employers and employees and suggested 'it is best to avoid gender specific prescriptive requirements, for example the requirement to wear high heels'.[27] Confused? So am I! Hopefully *you* get to decide whether you want to wear heels or not. The more women there are in power, the more opportunity we have to set the rules (or not have any at all).

Bags of style

Bags are another way to express our personality, complete our look and, of course, carry what we need for work. There is a lovely moment in *Working Girl* when Melanie Griffiths' character is given a gift of a beautiful briefcase by Harrison Ford, having claimed to have 'lost' the one she never had, as her explanation for carrying a tatty cardboard folder. I used to have a proper briefcase, full of papers for work. These days we are more likely to be lugging around a laptop, iPad, phone and chargers, along with gym kit, make-up, a hairbrush and house keys. For reasons of both form and function, few of us are still using a briefcase. Practicality is at least as important as the look, and it's best to avoid being weighed down by too many huge bags. There may actually be things that you *don't* need to keep carrying around. When working full-time at the same office, I started to notice that as the week went on, my workbag became heavier; I would just add things I needed each day rather than take out what was no longer required. I changed my ways after a journalist interviewed me about financial markets before asking for a business card. She then watched me fishing around in a huge, very messy bag, unable to locate a clean card. The story she wrote ended up being about how I wasn't so perfect after all (as if a messy bag was needed to prove that!) along with embarrassing details about the amount of junk I carried around (she caught me on a day when I even had a spare pair of flat shoes in my bag). Ever since, I've done a mid-week clear-out. I've also redefined what counts as 'essential' and downsized wherever possible, carrying a miniature hairbrush and the smallest number and size of any make-up items. This also helps when packing for short business trips, where my one essential tip is to travel as light as possible. Base your packing around one colour theme, one pair of smart but comfortable shoes and one versatile jacket and you'll be surprised how little you need.

I haven't always practised what I'm preaching. When I had a fixed desk in an office, I kept a few things under that desk. In my mind at least, it was a few items: spare tights, a couple of pairs of heels, gym shoes, clean gym kit in case I forgot it on a Pilates day. When I left the firm, I needed a large suitcase to carry everything home – there were five pairs of shoes, for a start! If you've no storage space in the office and can't fit what you need into a proper bag, don't be tempted to use plastic carrier bags (ever!). For her first job, Millie is using a neat black-and-cream backpack with a handle so that she can carry it as a handbag or on her back – it's functional yet looks smart and suitable for work (over-sized backpacks are more suited for a camping trip). Recycled cotton totes that can be folded up inside our main bag are a fall-back option for any extra items we pick up during the day – I have a strong black Planet Organic one that doesn't wreck the overall look of a dark outfit and is a positive talking point. A friend always carries *two* large smart leather bags, one over her shoulder and one held in the hand.

I used to have a sizeable collection of lovely bags for work, again amassed gradually over decades, until burglars stole most of them. I didn't replace them, realising that it was an opportunity to de-clutter and work out what was most useful. The burglars took only well-known labels (they knew their handbags) leaving me with a couple of elegant logo-free top-handle bags in neutral colours, the shiny black 'overnight case' I mentioned earlier and a bright orange classic handbag that is good at lifting subdued outfits and also works well with soft white. While the burglary was upsetting, it reminded me that less can be more. To vary the look of my diminished range I sometimes wind a scarf around a handle. I've been on the lookout for something similar to replace the one bag I really miss, a lovely capacious top-handle style with a cream outer layer that could be removed to reveal dark brown leather beneath – two looks in one and perfect for travelling light. The hunt itself has been quite fun, even if unsuccessful to date. As with so many aspects of our wardrobe, the 'perfect' work bag is a personal thing. I like sleek and structured large top-handle bags with plenty of room (and the strength) for an iPad but still feminine, even ladylike. Clearly that's not the only way to go. Suman Sidhu (exactly half my age) doesn't buy designer clothes but has invested in a large Louis Vuitton tote that she uses for work 'every single day'. She chose the bag in the label's subtle chequerboard print rather than the more obvious monogram. It's worth investing what you can on a versatile bag that you really love – although obviously that doesn't require breaking the bank on a designer label. Overt logos and blingy hardware are probably the only noes in an era when conspicuous consumption is out of fashion.

Watches and jewellery – avoid bling!

Similarly, there's no need to have a flashy watch or jewellery. In fact, I'd advise against it unless you work in 'luxury'. I know men who collect and wear very expensive watches that are presumably recognised by other aficionados, but that feels out of step with today's frugal times. Most people can't afford anything approaching these collectors' items, and it seems out of touch to parade them. One CEO that I know wears a beautiful but discreet gold Cartier watch – and she has just the one. Stylist Annie Castaño recommends that we do wear a watch at work – it looks rude to check our phone for the time in a meeting and a watch can be an extra 'point of interest' in our outfit. She stresses though that 'one good watch is plenty!' Mine is rose-gold, simple, unisex and vintage, with a brown leather strap; it's low key, something I've owned for many years and it seems to work with all my business outfits. But when it broke during lockdown, I borrowed my teenage daughter Octavia's inexpensive classic watch and grew very fond of it (yes I'm ashamed to say that I struggled to hand it back); we certainly don't need to wait until we can afford something special to buy a watch for work. Apart from too much bling, anything really goes: colleagues wear Apple watches, others have a favourite vintage, classic or sports watch.

Jangly, noisy jewellery is a no in almost every work situation (too distracting), but it doesn't have to be so delicate as to be invisible. US *Vogue* editor Anna Wintour always drapes multiple beautiful crystal necklaces around her neck whatever she's wearing, and as I write this, clunky neck chains are a 'thing', livening up plain tops on Zoom calls across the country. Dame Inga Beale, former CEO of Lloyd's of London – the first woman to hold the role – has always worn eclectic, dramatic jewellery, including rings with big stones in very unusual settings. Having admired her jewellery for years I only discovered quite recently that she is married to a Swiss jewellery designer. My own favourite item of jewellery is a brooch; brooches are often seen as old-fashioned, but I like to wear mine both classically and unexpectedly, perhaps at the close of a shirt or on a belt. My favourite has an interchangeable semi-precious centre stone, so I have collected a few different colours over the years and enjoy putting in one that works with the specific dress I'm wearing. My mother once remarked 'You're always wearing that brooch' which made me smile (even though she might not have meant it as a compliment); it's become my 'style signifier'.

Finishing touches – glasses, earrings and scarves

If we need them, glasses can be another hallmark of our business look. I am short-sighted and switch between contact lenses and tortoiseshell glasses – partly depending on just how I feel that day but also my overall look. I posted a pair of side-by-side, day-to-evening outfit pictures on Instagram: I wore glasses in the daytime look along with what appeared to be a plain black pencil skirt and fitted black-and-white tweed jacket, and then took off the jacket and glasses to reveal a little black dress with my signature brooch adorning the neckline. Even nerdy glasses can be ultra-cool these days, thanks to Gucci; I've just come off a Zoom call with a young blonde and brilliant female financial adviser, and she happened to be wearing oversized, thin-gold-rimmed spectacles that suited her face wonderfully and gave her a 'totally intelligent and totally cool' vibe. My friend and fellow 30% Club campaigner Tamara Box, the European managing partner of international top-20 law firm Reed Smith, has a vast collection of glasses, colour co-ordinated to match her outfits.

Earrings are another opportunity to experiment and to find a signature style – congresswoman AOC's hoops are not classic workwear, but they are integral to her overall sassy look. I often wear a pair of delicate Stephen Webster earrings that give the illusion of multiple piercings up my lobes – fun but fake news. A *Vogue* stylist even let me wear them with the outfit she'd picked out for me to wear on a workwear fashion shoot for the magazine – an endorsement, surely? Now, in the age of Zoom, earrings and necklaces are right up there, literally, as items to finish our on-screen look, along with scarves. A beautiful silk scarf can transform a plain round-necked T-shirt or sweater, and I've certainly been reaching more often for mine while working from home. But a classic silk scarf might be, well, too classic for your taste. McKinsey's Sundiatu Dixon-Fyle, a molecular biologist turned diversity and inclusion consultant, likes a more eclectic look and has discovered little-known Scandinavian brands such as Becksöndergaard on her business travels (and available online as well as at airports). These scarves are fine wool in amazing patterns and colours; in Sundiatu's words 'like a Hermes scarf in wool', only a lot less expensive. Draping one of these around her shoulders is now one of her signature looks: 'I'm known for my scarves.'

I usually wear a simple yet colourful dress for speaking events. At one such event in the City, a woman in the audience threw down a challenge: 'How can I wear colour? You're wearing a pink dress! I'm a lawyer and I couldn't even wear a pink scarf!' I questioned her assumption, how did she know that? She was a corporate lawyer, not a barrister where the rules around court dress are very restrictive. I asked had she ever considered *trying* and seeing what the reaction was? Afterwards over drinks, she agreed it was worth a try. A pink dress might feel too much in a traditional environment, but a pink scarf? What could really go wrong? If you're unsure about how to add some feminin- ity and personality to your look, accessories are the perfect place to start.

Having completed your outfit, found your speaking voice and sorted out your hair and make-up, it's time to switch gears. We've been focusing up to this point on the ways you present yourself at work. We now need to look at what lies beneath the surface – not your technical knowledge (which is out of scope here), but how you feel, take care of yourself and manage life events so that you are centred, calm and can concentrate well. These are all essential elements of sustained career success. Given the toll taken by the pandemic, we're going to start with the specific issues related to working from home and managing your work–life balance.

Takeaways from Chapter 6

1. Accessories are a great way to pull an outfit together and to create different looks from the same clothes. They can be a good way to start pushing out your style frontiers at work. You can start to introduce your personality into a conventional outfit with a colourful scarf, interesting brooch or earrings, unusual shoes, cool glasses or bag.

2. Wearing high heels should be a personal choice. If they make you feel more authoritative, wear them, but if you feel better in flats, that's fine, too.

3. The right bag for you is one that is functional *and* works with your outfits. Make sure it is big enough for your everyday needs but don't carry excess clutter. The only no in an era where conspicuous consumption looks out of touch is anything overtly expensive, flashy or 'designer'. Discreet, high-quality bags can upgrade everything else in your wardrobe.

4. Similarly, blingy, very obviously expensive watches are out of sync with the era; just one good watch is plenty, but if you can't afford your 'perfect' watch, anything that reflects your character – sporty, classic or a 'smart' watch – is just fine. It's useful to wear a watch to avoid having to check your phone for the time.

5. The pandemic has changed the focus from shoes and handbags to scarves, necklaces and earrings. If you are working in a hybrid way, you'll need a few of each – but less can be more. High-quality items that you love are better for both uplifting high street or very simple clothes and for the environment.

Chapter 7

Winning in the Zoom Age:
How to Work Successfully at Home

'This digital world is what you make of it
in the end.'

Ciara, American singer-songwriter

All our lives were turned upside down by COVID-19, but the impact was not felt equally. After years of progress towards gender equality at work, women's employment and career prospects suffered a disproportionate setback. The divergence happened almost immediately. During the first lockdown, mothers in the UK were 47 per cent more likely than fathers to have lost their job (or quit) and 14 per cent more likely to have been furloughed.[28] With schools closed and no household help, those able to work from home struggled to balance paid work with significantly increased childcare and domestic duties – and the burden did not fall evenly. Mothers managed just one hour of uninterrupted work for every three that fathers did during the first lockdown (even though men also stepped up their child-care hours).[29] A friend of mine who's built a successful career over three decades told me she had to stop working during lockdown to keep her family going: her husband had recently started a new role and they concluded it was the only way to ensure at least one of their careers survived. For many families, it's been financially logical to prioritise fathers' typically higher-paying jobs. A year on from the start of lockdowns, McKinsey looked back at the cumulative damage, suggesting that 'while all women have been impacted, three major groups have experienced some of the largest challenges: working mothers (especially those with children under ten), women in senior management positions (over 50 per cent reported feeling consistently 'exhausted') and black women (people of colour in the US cited 'acute challenges' over career progression and household responsibilities more than twice as often as white Americans).[30] 'Survival' became the goal for many women caught up in an impossible juggling act.

As we look to recover – personally, professionally and soci-etally – there is much to learn from these experiences. The circumstances of the pandemic were stressful and *in*flexible: for many, it felt less like 'working from home' than 'living at work'. To accommodate the combined load of domestic and 'real' work, our day simply stretched: we started work-ing earlier and kept working later. Online behaviour suggests that American workers added three hours to their working day, compared with two hours in France, Spain and the UK. But for all the stresses and strains, the experience proved in practice what had been impossible to prove in theory: we can be productive anywhere, subject only to a decent Internet connection and laptop (surprise, surprise!). A year after the first lockdown, more than two-thirds (70 per cent) of British employers said that the pandemic-induced increase in homeworking either boosted or made no difference to productivity.[31] That's a big shift in perceptions: before the pandemic, working from home ('shirking from home') was seen as a soft option, usually granted to mothers as a perk. Today, even the most workaholic CEO sees that remote working can be both efficient and cost-effective. Yet working full-time at home isn't ideal, either: we miss the interactions that naturally occur in the office, the camaraderie, the sparks that lead to new ideas and the many opportunities to learn from others, particularly early on in our careers. And while working from home may be appealing if you share a lovely house and big garden with your family, it can be quite miserable for those in crowded shared accommodation or living alone. (Note: if you really struggle to work remotely, request an exemption from any working from home policy. As long as your company has an office, they should be willing to make a special case – there is generally now a good understanding about mental health and other problems that may arise.)

While *full-time* working from home isn't going to be feasible for most businesses or people, it's just as clear that traditional five-long-days-a-week-in-the-same-office working practices are outdated, expensive (high real-estate costs), exhausting (long commutes), unnecessary (lots of tasks are better suited to home-working) and exclusive (there are limited opportunities for those who can't afford, or don't want, to live in big cities).

So, where do we go from here?

The new working environment

Now that the genie is out of the bottle, hybrid working – mixing days in the office (to build team rapport and informal

communications) with days at home (for expediency and balanced lives) – is becoming the norm for many. But successful
and enjoyable working from home doesn't just happen automatically – it's a skill. If we're going to forge ahead, we need to
understand how to get a job, keep that job, perform well, stay
visible and be heard in an online environment. That strong personal brand matters just as much – if not more so – when we're
working virtually, with fewer levers at our disposal to make an
impact. There are few experts in navigating this digital world;
the good news is that we can learn techniques to give us an edge.

First and foremost, our working practices need to be
sustainable.

One of my mentees, a senior woman managing a large team,
explained that during lockdown, she was on video calls from 8am
till 8pm each day with barely any respite. She found herself over-
reacting to a series of (work-related) issues one day and sought
my advice about dealing with the pressures. I told her that she
was bound to feel on edge unless she shortened her working day,
insisted on gaps in the diary and used those times to get fresh air
and exercise. She said everyone 'wanted a piece of her'. I pushed
back: no one can run on empty – especially over long periods of
time – she needed to make it clear that she couldn't be always
available. From her company's perspective, remote working has
been fantastic: the CEO is considering drastically reducing the
office space. With home-working here to stay for at least a significant portion of her week, my mentee needs to consciously change
her approach to avoid burnout.

Here's how to work successfully – and happily – from home,
whether you're doing it five days a week or mixing days at home
with days in the office.

Create boundaries and optimise what you have

It is essential to create boundaries. Designate a workspace, ideally somewhere comfortable with natural light. Treat it as a proper office and get the basics right; make sure that you have a desk or table at a good height, a chair that doesn't make your back ache, a socket to charge your devices and a decent WiFi or broadband connection. It's stressful working at home with a poor signal. Many of my younger colleagues working on the Diversity Project live in flatshares with limited connectivity and very little space; one explained that she and her flatmates had a booking system for the best (really the only) place for important online meetings. They had also shared the expense of upgrading their WiFi to avoid arguments about anyone monopolising the connection. Another young friend in his twenties lives alone, with good space and WiFi but has very limited human contact when working from home, creating a temptation to work all day and night. He has designated one room as his 'office' and sticks to a routine. If your work area is also used as a living space by other members of your household, make it clear when you are working by assigning 'office hours' or simply closing the door when you can't be disturbed. If there's no door (the downside of the recent trend towards open-plan living), ensure that everyone else at home knows when you can't be interrupted. I shared 'office' space with two of my university-student children while we were all working from home during lockdowns. The prime spot (best background, WiFi signal *and* usually the quietest room) had to be booked for important meetings or tutorials, and if extra quiet was needed for a webinar, lesson or exam, we stuck a 'Do not disturb' sign on the door. I was just about to log on to speak at a major event with over 1,000 attendees when Bea mentioned that she was about to start her drum lesson in the room next door. We negotiated and she ended up having a rather strange, silent drum lesson that day! If you really struggle to create physical boundaries in your home, it's even more important to set *time* boundaries by having a routine.

Create a routine

Wake up at the same time each morning (and treat weekends and holidays differently). Shower, do your hair and make-up, get properly dressed. Sometimes I have to steel myself to go through the whole routine, especially ahead of a groundhog dawn-to-dusk Zoomday, but if I don't, I'll feel mentally as well as physically unwashed. If you have difficult tasks, tackle them at your peak time of the day – I'm a morning person, so I try to do my most challenging work first thing. Allocate some time to admin, however boring that might seem. If you aren't on top of your meeting schedule or planning properly for major pieces of work, chaos and stress *will* follow. Don't check emails constantly or you'll never get anything done; have certain times of the day when you go through your inbox (two or three times a day at most). Ask people to WhatsApp, text or call you about anything urgent so that you don't need to worry about missing something. (It drives me crazy that people assume we've read an email just because they sent it.) Take a break for lunch and *make* time (even just half an hour) for fresh air and exercise, ideally in the middle of the day to break up the monotony and physical strain of sitting in front of a screen. My young friend who lives alone took up running during the first lockdown and stops working when he's at home for an hour-long daily run. I walk Buddy late morning, and, if time is short, we run together (I'll decide between 60-,

45- or 30-minute routes/speeds). If you have children at home, create a routine for them as well, including times when you are available to help them or simply to talk. In 'normal' times (that is, when not home-schooling), building the school run into your own schedule can be a wonderful opportunity to catch up on your child's day. Although she's increasingly keen to come home by herself, I love collecting my youngest daughter Bea from school – she's always cheerful and gregarious. We have a lovely chat on the journey home and then I make a cup of tea while she enjoys a snack before I resume my work and she starts her homework. In the evening, we'll relax together as a family; several of us will play a game like Bananagrams just before supper and we'll watch TV after we've cleared the table. Some of us might have to go back to work later in the evening, but the basic framework is there to help pace ourselves. Of course, it's not always possible to stick to the exact same routine – don't make it an added stress factor, just try to keep to it as much as possible.

Sort out your video call set-up to help you feel confident

It took me several attempts to create the right set-up, but now it's done I can relax about the whole thing. Some people recommend a plain backdrop; I think that looks too clinical, like a prison cell (although see the exception on page 151 when we consider asynchronous video job interviews). There's always the fake-background option, but unless you position yourself perfectly and sit very still, there's a risk of being cut off as you move around – it's a little disconcerting watching someone fade in and out. A blurred backdrop makes me wonder if the person has something to hide (am I the only one thinking that?). The remaining options are either a screen with a logo if you have access to one (very corporate, but good for company meetings) or your actual home, which is preferable – it just needs a little thought. You want to give your colleagues insights that tell them what you *want* them to know. We might have sat next to someone in the office for years but learned very little about them. Ironically, since we've been working remotely, the glimpses into our colleagues' homes and family lives have created more human connections. We've probably all experienced the occasional embarrassing moment; Buddy barks loudly when the doorbell rings, which all too often coincides with my first attempt to speak. The interruption seems (mostly) to create a welcome moment of light relief on the call. There are other (quieter) talking points; one colleague has a giant glued-together jigsaw puzzle of a battle scene behind her; the picture is very Old Master, the jigsaw makes it fascinating. I've noticed that Zoom meetings often start with comments on new backdrops (perhaps because we've so few other excitements). At a recent important meeting, the chairman spent the first few minutes enquiring about the snowy scene behind one participant. She'd photographed her garden and made it into a very effective (if chilly-looking) backdrop. My favourite spot is to sit in front of a wall covered in wallpaper designed to look like a giant bookshelf – it looks as though I have a great many books and is a good ice-breaker as people try to work it out. There's also no danger of offending anyone with my reading material (remember to check the titles of real books displayed as well as any photographs you'd rather not share).

Never sit in front of a window, unless you draw the blind or curtains, as the bright light shining behind you will leave you silhouetted and hard to see. This is critical for video interviews that might be assessed by an algorithm: the programme might be analysing your facial expressions, eye movements, the way your lips move. If your features can't be seen properly, that's a problem. The light needs to be in front of you – either natural light or a desk lamp. There are special lights devised for working-from-home set-ups. I have an Elgato lamp, which is adjustable (for height, angle, brightness and tint) and it makes a big difference, giving a helpful glow. One of my daughters uses a ring light, which diffuses light evenly and is often used for close-up photographs. Remember, you can test out how things look – it's very easy to just set up an instant Zoom 'new meeting' and see what others will see before you join the real call. I appeared on Sky News in my usual working-from-home spot, wearing a simple short-sleeved cream dress and gold chain necklace. A few moments earlier I'd tried it out, only to see that the dress looked creased around the arms and I didn't look in the least authoritative. I grabbed a plain navy cardigan and suddenly the whole thing worked. Afterwards someone sent me a message saying I 'looked great' on the programme (although I'm not sure she remembered what I'd actually said).

Get the camera angle right

Your camera needs to be at eye level. Many people look down at their computer, but that creates a double chin. I perch my computer on a wooden box or books; anything that forms a stable base. The distance you sit from the camera is also something to consider. You don't want to loom gigantically on-screen, nor do you want to be way off in the distance. Make sure that there isn't acres of space above your head in the picture, too – I've often found my screen needs to be tilted down so that the camera angle gives a more balanced image. I've done several TV appearances via Zoom; the producer always works to get me centred in the frame. Just play around with the set-up until it looks natural and as if you are talking to someone across the desk rather than across the Internet. Ensure your hand movements can be seen; we have a reduced range of communication online and hand gestures can help you appear animated and engaged. Work out how to appear as if you are looking at the other person; that might not be the same as looking directly at them on-screen. The camera on my iPad is on the left, in the middle. It's quite tricky to remember to look there, so I stick a tiny Post-it note with an arrow on my screen. One disadvantage with 'Teams' if someone is screen-sharing is that the participants are shown along the bottom of the screen, so if we look down at them (as it's natural to do) our eyes appear half-closed. The camera on the iPad is good quality; my previous laptop made me very grainy. If I hadn't needed a new device I'd have invested in a special camera to attach to the top of the old one. Logitech webcams are very popular for video meetings and they also automatically correct any lighting problems.

Dress for online

Don't worry, we're not going to have to start all over again! Here are just a few extra tips for dressing for success online. Number one: never, ever wear pyjamas – at least not the full set. A British *Vogue* feature on 'The Ultimate Working from Home Wardrobe' took waist-up dressing to extremes: structured jackets and glamorous pussy-bow blouses worn with tracksuit and pyjama bottoms, leggings, shorts and fluffy slippers. The caption to one picture read 'Who knows what she has on from the waist down?' It's true that no one would ever know. When I spoke to Suman Sidhu on Zoom about her 'style and substance' she looked very glamorous, in an unusual V-neck top with gathered

sleeves, beautiful shiny hair and make-up. Suman took delight
in showing me that she was wearing joggers on her lower half.
It's a personal choice: I need sartorial boundaries between 'home
clothes' and 'work clothes' and would feel a bit strange having
such a disconnect between my top and bottom attire, but perhaps
that's just me!

At the same time, it's usually unnecessary to wear a formal
jacket – after all, everyone knows that you are working from
home. I tend to wear simple smartish tops (my current favourite
is a fine-knit orchid-pink short-sleeved cardigan with a pussy-
bow neckline) and relaxed trousers (the pink cardigan works
with a much-loved cream pair or my favourite jeans). There are
only a few other don'ts for online meetings: no frills, no busy
tight patterns that might look psychedelic on-screen, and take
care with black and white. Even if it suits you in real life, bright
white is harsh on-screen and black can be draining, depending
on your skin tone. Many of us have resorted to classic black
Audrey Hepburn-style polo necks; they are chic, comfortable
and easy to wear, but check that you haven't inadvertently created a floating head effect, especially if your background is dark.
One of my fellow members of the House of Lords, Baroness
Buscombe, went viral after giving a speech, with her perfect floating head likened to both Holly from sci-fi sitcom *Red Dwarf* and
Queen's *Bohemian Rhapsody* cover. She garnered attention but
probably not in the way she wanted. The best clothes for video-
conferencing are the ones that we're also advised to wear on TV:
necklines that frame your face (all those pussy bows), warm block
colours (I once appeared on an all-female panel on *Newsnight*;
the four of us were wearing various shades of pink and orange),
covered shoulders (sleeveless is fine in summer), neat shapes.
I'd consigned a number of coloured shift dresses to the back of
my wardrobe a few years before the pandemic, feeling that they

were a bit dated, but having seen a colleague look fabulous on a Zoom call in her light pink one early on in lockdown, I took mine out again. I often wear them with a necklace or my brooch, while taking care not to have anything very distracting near my face (dangly earrings might work for a creative Instagram Live session but not so well for my formal corporate board meetings). Just take a look at the overall effect before you start that important meeting, as the image staring back at you might not be quite what you have in your mind. You're not seeking perfection, just a look that makes you feel confident and lets you focus on the meeting itself.

Reassess your make-up

TV presenters tend to wear extra make-up on-air, partly because of the bright studio lighting. Our lighting at home is less predictable, so do a quick Zoom-call rehearsal to see how you look before joining an important call. (Remember, Zoom has a 'touch up my appearance' option under 'meeting settings' and you can have it 'always on'. I love that function!) Prepare your skin well: an exhausted face seems more noticeable on Zoom. After a video meeting at the end of a long day a friend called to ask whether I was feeling OK. I'd not slept well the night before and knew I looked tired, but I hadn't compensated with extra make-up. The little cosmetic case on my working-from-home desk includes powder (video makes us shinier), concealer, a couple of eye shadows and liner, lipstick and a mirror, so I can quickly check my make-up and touch up during the day even when doing back-to-backs. Lipstick colour can look quite different on-screen, so don't just stick to what you've always used. I've ended up toning down even my nude shade, as my usual choice looked brighter on video. Some (usually much younger) colleagues have dialled up their lip colour, making that more of a trademark – and showing that they are making an effort. Whatever you decide, do *not* join a call with unbrushed or unwashed hair, no make-up and looking as though you've given up. Over the pandemic, it hasn't been possible to control many aspects of our lives, but we can still control our image. That might seem unimportant in the context of a crisis, but as we look to recover from what has truly been a testing time, it will stand us in good stead for the next phase of our lives and careers. It doesn't mean looking robotically perfect, it means showing you respect your colleagues, respect yourself and are trying your best. Those who continue making an effort after over a year of working from home really make a positive impression. Earlier today I chaired a big conference call. The group meets once a month and one woman always stands out, with red lipstick, carefully brushed glossy dark hair and great earrings. In an office, she might be less noticeable, but she is using the opportunity to make an impact on the screen. By contrast, a couple of attendees look as if they have lost heart – I feel more concerned than judgemental. If one day you really have no time (or energy) for even basic grooming, brush your hair and put it in a neat ponytail (or whatever style works best for your low-maintenance days) and reach for the concealer, powder and either lipstick or whatever makes you feel presentable. Two minutes is all it will take to go from unkempt to orderly. And spray on a little perfume to help relax your mind and create a nice atmosphere – even if you are the only one who will benefit.

Over-communicate: show you are engaged

One of the disadvantages of working remotely is that it's harder
to be visible. 'Out of sight, out of mind' applies whatever your
level of seniority. One company told me that they'd conducted a
staff survey at the end of 2020. The management team was disappointed to receive a very clear message that they hadn't been
'visible' during the crisis. They had stepped up communications –
but not nearly enough. As individuals, we face a similar risk. Be
proactive in showing that you are engaged, ask your manager
for one-to-one time if they don't offer it, participate verbally in
online meetings (and be involved in the written 'chat'). Keep your
camera on whenever possible and exhibit enthusiasm. Since we
can't walk the floor when we're working from home, we need to
use other methods of communication outside meetings. We're
in danger of becoming 'Zoombies', drained after hours in front
of our screens. A simple old-fashioned voice call to a colleague
can feel strangely refreshing. Reach out to colleagues you might
previously have just bumped into every now and again – just for
a chat. Those informal water-cooler moments can still happen,
just not around the water cooler itself. To create a more level
playing field and avoid everyone piling into the office on the same
days as the boss, some companies are using video conferencing
for *all* meeting participants whether they are in the office or at
home. Ideally, everyone is mixing and matching working at home
and in the office, so it becomes a shared way of life. If you are
working predominantly or completely from home, make extra
sure that you are consciously still building or maintaining relationships with colleagues. If you are working for a company that
has decided not to have a physical office at all, suggest occasional
real-life get-togethers. And remember to keep building your

external network, too. While this can be done remotely through social media or online events, keep a look out for opportunities to socialise in person with those who might be able to open doors or simply offer advice and encouragement.

Master video-conferencing etiquette

Meetings work differently online. The good news is that we all have one equally shaped tile on the gallery view and can raise our virtual hand. It's intrinsically egalitarian, contrasting with in-person meetings where even the seating arrangement can convey a status hierarchy. There's probably still a hierarchy among participants in a video call, but you don't need to be the loudest voice in the room or seek a rare opportunity to get a word in edgeways – you can simply raise your hand. Take that opportunity! Don't hog the microphone, but do get stuck into the conversation. Online, it's harder for the chair to draw people in who aren't actively participating, especially when there's a large number on the call. I chaired a meeting with over 30 participants and someone complained afterwards that they hadn't been able to get involved in the conversation – but they never raised their hand. When you do make a point, make it clearly: you have fewer ways to make an impression – you can't reinforce a confident voice through your body language, for example. It's also hard to read the room. A mentee said she was concerned that people might be 'inwardly' rolling their eyes or exchanging negative feedback about her via email or WhatsApp. I told her to banish such misgivings and concentrate instead on making her contributions the very best they could be. You'll be able to impress in regular online meetings if you have good ideas, are prepared to speak up and have your set-up arranged in advance so that you're confident about that. It takes practice to do a good formal presentation online. Make sure you know how to share your screen (and make it full size) and if you're giving a long talk, see if there are ways to make it interactive at points, to avoid it becoming a monologue. I've often started longer online talks with a polling question, getting my audience involved right from the start. As with a real-life presentation, we need to put ourselves in our listeners' place. How can you raise their level of interest in what you're saying? Don't rule out judicious use of humour. In November 2020, the Diversity Project held its usual annual seminar online for the first time. We wanted to include a section on (the lack of) gender balance in the investment industry. It's a well-worn subject, and a classic panel discussion might have prompted the audience to reach for the 'leave meeting' button. The solution? To commission a comedienne to reframe the issue; to be a bit self-deprecating and poke a little fun at ourselves as well as the system we're trying to change. I was nervous; there's a lot that can go wrong with comedy, so we discussed the script many times with our chosen performer, Elf Lyons, and pre-recorded the sketch to avoid surprises. It was worth the risk; the sketch was unexpected, sustained people's attention – and made them laugh.

One type of online meeting needs specific preparation: video job interviews. We'll come back to that in a moment.

Resolve any physical strains

Monitor how you're feeling. If your back aches, eyes feel strained or you develop a regular headache, it's important to address the problem. My middle son was struggling with eye strain while studying online but has found a solution in wearing blue-light-blocking glasses – easily available and inexpensive. Blue light from laptops is also thought to cause sleep and anxiety issues. Even if the science isn't proven, the glasses are worth a try if you suffer from headaches, eye strain or difficulty switching off at night. Headaches are often stress-related, linked to eye strain or a sign of dehydration; again, don't just hope the problem corrects itself, check that you are drinking enough water, take an eye test and try to exercise more to relieve any stress. My upper back ached terribly when I first started working full-time at home. The chair was too high for the table, and I was stooping. When I swapped the chair for a lower one and remembered to stand up regularly to stretch, the ache disappeared.

Make the weekends count

If you're working from home full-time, life can feel like one long continuum. Create punctuation points, leave your desk for the day or weekend, put an 'out of office' auto reply on for emails and (if possible) put your phone in a drawer, spend time with your family and friends, and celebrate special moments. Dr Cary Cooper, author of *Wellbeing at Work*, expresses perfectly what we learned through lockdown: 'What this health crisis has done is make people reflect on the fact that life is a one-act play.' There is no second act, so we need to make the first and only act as good as it can be – whatever the circumstances. Lockdown wore so many of us down with the monotony, made worse by loneliness, cramped living space or mental health problems. With few opportunities to do anything more exciting than a local walk, our family made a diary of upcoming festivals and celebrated them *all*, especially in winter. One particularly indulgent week in February included Chinese New Year (celebrated with a home-cooked Chinese banquet), Valentine's Day (lots of heart-shaped balloons, a special cake, roses, pink sparkling wine and little gifts for each other) and Pancake Day (lots of pancake tossing and eating, obviously). Our home-made festivities certainly livened up the long, dark evenings and helped us enjoy each other's company rather than be at each other's throats at the end of a long day of home-schooling, university and work. The only downside is that fun weekends made it harder to feel motivated on Mondays, but we decided that it was better to deal with that than not have any fun at all!

Video job interviews

Of course, mastering working from home is only useful if you have a job in the first place. In an increasingly competitive digitalised world, there are new challenges to overcome to succeed at interview. In earlier chapters, we discussed the value of open body language, the ability to connect with others and confidence in your appearance as you enter a room. We lose many of these ways to create a good impression online, so the task can seem even more daunting. But if you're aware of the limitations and, as always, you use what you do have, exciting possibilities will beckon, so let's take a look at how to make it through video job interviews.

There are several types of video interview, including those that involve a live conversation with a real person. This requires similar preparation to an in-person interview, just adapted for the online setting. This type of interview seems to create a more level playing field for women. I have plenty of experience being rejected for roles after in-person interviews but an almost 100 per cent success rate via video. I've compared notes with female friends and we've all fared better online. The main pitfall is a temptation to fill any gaps in the conversation. If you've answered the question and the interviewer hasn't yet thought of the next one, pause and wait. As part of a panel, I recently interviewed candidates for a prestigious role. There was just one woman in the five-strong shortlist and to my great disappointment, the male interviewers all thought she had 'waffled'. I thought she was brilliant, but it was hard to counter their argument: when in doubt, she had carried on speaking. But, generally, this is an equalising forum for us since any potential awkwardness between a man and a woman pretty much disappears over video. Interviewers aren't always men, of course, but in my case, working in financial services, they usually are. I've been able to strike up a rapport much more quickly talking to men who I might find a little intimidating (or who might think the same about me!) if we were to meet in real life. We just get on with the conversation. The only specific preparation needed is to spend some time on the practicalities: charge your device, check your set-up, connection and appearance in a practice call, ensure your slides load quickly and easily if you're going to do a presentation, and that you're in a quiet place where you won't be interrupted.

A live online conversation with another person is becoming a rarity for first interviews for entry or mid-level roles in large companies. Even before COVID-19, over 60 per cent of large American corporations used video recruitment technology involving pre-recorded questions.[32] During the pandemic, that increased to 86 per cent – and the number keeps rising,[33] while the trend is spreading globally. The benefits for companies are obvious; an automated recruitment process is efficient, cheaper and enables them to process more applications. Many candidates also like the faster turnaround times, the convenience of recording interviews when it suits and the greater chance of having an interview at all – but the format can be disconcerting, especially if you don't know what to expect.

The asynchronous video interview

An asynchronous video interview is like a one-way Zoom call. You are usually given a window of time to record yourself – say within 48 hours after being invited to interview. When the 'interview' starts, you'll be prompted by a series of questions or instructions (often in a video while also displayed as text on the screen), such as 'introduce yourself and tell us about your background and experience'. You'll usually be given a couple of minutes to prepare a short response and told how long the response should be – it might be just 30 seconds – then speak to the camera. Programmes often allow you to practise your answers, but you'll usually get just one attempt at the actual recording. You probably won't know the specific questions in advance, but some will be personal and behavioural; for example, 'Give me a time when something didn't go to plan and describe how you responded', others are more technical, related to the job you are applying for. It's an intrinsically unnatural situation: there are no follow-up questions, no responses to your answers – not even an acknowledgement. The key is to practise until you feel used to the format; think of the questions as an exercise rather than a conversation. Some platforms do also set puzzles, games or an exercise to complete. As with traditional interviews, do your homework around the company and the role you are applying for, and think about how you will respond to challenges such as 'Tell us about your greatest strength' or 'Tell us about how you resolved a conflict with a more senior colleague.' An obvious difference from an interview with a real person is that you don't get a chance to engage in conversation and for your answer to unfold; it has to be succinct and your language less tentative (if you have a tendency to muse, saying 'I think' a lot, it's best to try to leave that out).

Many interview coaches recommend adopting the 'STAR' framework for your answers: describe the Situation, the Task, the Action and the Results. It takes a bit of getting used to, but the structure helps to keep answers concise and to the point:

Question:
'Give me a time when something didn't go to plan and describe how you responded.'

Answer:
I was leading a team working on an important advertising brief but at the eleventh hour the client rejected it. (Situation)

We had to go back to the drawing board – and fast – because the advertising space had already been booked. (Task)

I consulted further with the client around what they didn't like about the proposal and developed a better understanding of what they were looking for. (Action)

I discussed the revised brief with the team, and everyone agreed to work over the weekend to come up with a second proposal. The client was happy and we made the copy deadlines. (Result)

The answer is short on detail but clear-cut, it shows determination, responsiveness, leadership (it's important the example shows personal accountability) and good teamwork.

My daughter-in-law, Dyedra, undertook several recorded video interviews mid-pandemic in her efforts to find her first role outside academia. The video interviews were often the third stage in the process, after the written application and a series of online aptitude tests. Dyedra prepared extensively for each interview: she had a bank of possible answers ready, organised as bullet points by topic, so that she could use the allotted preparation time to organise her thoughts. (She didn't read the answers though – that would have been too mechanical.) She also researched the different programmes to better understand how her interview would be evaluated. Some platforms (HireVue, for example) are heavily dependent on artificial intelligence (AI), others such as Visiotalent declare 'Technology should be at the service of humans and not replace them.' The Visiotalent interviews are 'always watched by real recruiters whose evaluation of candidates is their expertise'. Getting past any algorithm-based assessment will usually be just one stage in any application process. You should assume that if your video passes that test, it will be watched by a real person before you're invited to the next round.

Dyedra wore what she'd normally wear for an interview (sometimes there's specific guidance; Goldman Sachs suggests 'business casual') and ensured that there was good lighting and WiFi in the room where she was recording. She kept the background as plain as possible, since books and pictures can distract the computer programme. Dyedra speaks with a German accent and was concerned that this might be a disadvantage; one significant drawback of automated interviews is that there's no feedback, so she will never know why she passed some and not others. Her hit rate improved as she did more interviews and became accustomed to the format, more relaxed and therefore able to show her personality. In her first recorded interviews, for example, Dyedra was consciously using technical expressions relevant to each company. She soon realised it was better to demonstrate certain strengths and behaviours rather than trying to show off specific knowledge that the AI system wasn't necessarily trained to pick up. Once she spoke more naturally, her success rate improved. In the end, Dyedra accepted a great job with a small company who interviewed her through (online) conversations with actual people. She wasn't put off by the AI interviews, but it was certainly easier to get a feel for the company and its culture through discussions with real prospective colleagues.

Which system is better? Author Malcolm Gladwell believes that human beings are terrible at predicting who will perform well in a job from interviews and CVs. He suggests that all hiring is effectively arbitrary.[34] Those of us who've been through many job interviews as both interviewer and interviewee will concede that it's often very subjective. Brilliant people can perform poorly at interview; a weak candidate can shine. Often it seems impossible to know who will perform best at the job, especially when all the shortlisted candidates have relevant technical expertise and experience. Besides performance at interview, the decision over who to make the offer to – and in turn a candidate's decision to accept – is often based on personal chemistry and empathy.

When first launched, there was great hope that AI-based assessments could eliminate human biases and make hiring fairer. In 2014, Amazon started building its own automated hiring programmes for top talent. By the following year, it became clear that the new system was biased towards recruiting men for software developer and other technical jobs – because most of those already hired for those roles were men. In effect, Amazon's system taught itself that male candidates were preferable and penalised applicants who had, for example, attended an all-women college. The word 'women' was automatically interpreted by the programme as a negative. Amazon edited the software to neutralise obviously gendered words but couldn't guarantee that it wouldn't still have subtler biases, so ultimately it abandoned the effort.

Despite ongoing attempts to eliminate both gender and racial biases from AI-based programmes, the concerns are entirely logical. If machines learn from the past, and past success has been dominated by white men from a narrow social and educational background, surely AI will perpetuate, not correct the problem?

Such concerns haven't dented employers' enthusiasm for using video recruitment tools. HireVue is a popular platform used by many large prestigious employers, including investment banks. The system develops a profile for each role based on aptitudes, experiences and behaviours deemed ideal for that particular job, and candidates are judged against that profile. Different parameters are set for each industry, company and role. Being empathetic is an important characteristic for a role in healthcare, for example, but might not be so relevant for an engineering job. The algorithms adapt and learn as new data is gathered. In 2021 HireVue announced that it had stopped using facial expressions as a factor after the company's own research suggested that 'visual analysis no longer significantly added value' because of advances in language analysis. Its interviews are still analysed on the basis of as many as 15,000 factors, including choice of words and voice intonation. The system is interested not just in the actual answers but in *what's going on below the surface*. The programmes are designed so that they can't be gamed.

Although it might seem odd to be speaking to a computer programme, the key to success is to act as close to your normal self as possible. As Aida Fazylova, CEO of HR tech start-up XOR, which automates preliminary hiring stages, suggests, 'If you want to ace your screening interview with AI, I'd recommend a heavy dose of honesty, values and personality.'[35] A natural performance means speaking as you usually do at your regular pace, having a good but not exaggerated level of enthusiasm, looking into the camera but not with a fixed stare (it's fine to look away when you need to, just like in a face-to-face interview), using the language you would normally use, pausing, breathing, smiling ... all good common sense. Set up your device, then record yourself giving mock answers to plausible questions. Play them back and keep practising until you are happy that you don't feel, look or sound fazed by the technology. The good news is that these one-way interviews tend to be shorter than they would be with a person – perhaps 25 minutes. Twenty-five minutes to be clear, concise, consistent and naturally confident. You can do that!

Once you land the role, you can put into practice all that we've covered so far. Starting a new role is exciting, and we tend to throw ourselves into it – rightly so. But sometimes the pace is simply unsustainable. We've covered the danger of not switching off when working from home; it's time to consider more generally how we manage our time and health to sustain our careers over the long term. We can put our 'best foot forward' for interviews, but building and sustaining a multi-decade career demands stamina, and that requires us to take good care of ourselves in the context of the many different challenges and time constraints we might experience. That's not just possible, but *necessary* if we are to fulfil our career potential.

Takeaways from Chapter 7

1. Successful working from home requires a distinct approach compared with working in a physical office.

2. It's important to create boundaries between 'working from home' and 'living at home' – ideally (if space allows) both physical and time boundaries. If your 'office' doubles up as a living area, ensure that those time boundaries are in place. If you share space with other workers at home, have a booking system for the prime location.

3. Spend time and effort sorting out the practicalities: the right background (gives a glimpse of your personality); the height of your desk and chair (be comfortable); the lighting (the window or light needs to be in front); the camera angle and height (eye level, not too much headspace); the distance you sit from the screen (the aim is to look as if you are across the desk from your online colleagues); and of course the Internet connection.

4. Adapt your clothes for online, focusing on your top half while ensuring that your whole outfit helps you get into the right mindset for work. Some of us need sartorial boundaries as well as those around space and time. Colours can look different on-screen – use the 'new meeting' function on Zoom to see the 'you' you're presenting to colleagues ahead of the actual meeting. Scarves, jackets, necklaces, earrings, can all transform a basic jumper or T-shirt into something more suitable for a work meeting.

5. Reassess your make-up to take account of the lighting. You might need a little extra, or to tone colours down. Keep a small cosmetics case to hand for touch-ups especially

→

during a busy day. Use Zoom's 'touch up my appearance' for an easy boost.

6. Ensure you have breaks and use them for fresh air. Sort out any physical ailments – stretch more, adjust your desk or chair if you get backache. Drink plenty of water during the day. Try blue-light-blocking glasses if you suffer from eye strain.

7. Devise a strategy to avoid being 'out of sight, out of mind', especially if other colleagues are office based. Be visible and engaged in meetings. Keep your camera on. Reach out to colleagues for catch-ups even if there's no formal requirement.

8. Make the most of the egalitarian format of video conferencing – you have an equally sized tile and access to the 'raise your hand' button. Use them to the full.

9. Switch off at weekends and in the evenings; create punctuation points.

10. Video job interviewing is quite different from real-life interviews. Asynchronous (one-way, recorded) interviews take time getting used to. The more you can practise and feel at ease, the better you'll come across. These interviews are usually short and intense, and you can schedule them to suit. Be open, honest and clear in your answers, and don't try to second-guess the algorithm – it'll show. Ironically, the key is to be natural.

Chapter 8

Sustaining and Fuelling Your Career: Finding Time to Take Care of Yourself

> 'Most of us spend too much time on what is urgent and not enough time on what is important.'
>
> *Stephen Covey, author of*
> The 7 Habits of Highly Effective People

My boss in New York had a two-and-a-half-hour commute from his home in New Jersey and yet would arrive in the office at 7am sharp each morning. His wife drove him to the train station *every weekday* at 4.30am (I still can't quite get my head around that). He would bound into the office and expect an immediate run-down of the Asian and European markets. As a novice, this took me a while to prepare. I desperately wanted to please him, so I set my alarm clock earlier and earlier before finally settling into a regime where I would be at my desk by 6am with a full hour to read up on overnight developments. There were just the two of us in the 'team', plus a wonderful assistant. Very quickly, my role expanded to cover everything from trading (buying or selling bonds over the phone), settling the trades (transferring bonds or money), sorting out trades that 'failed' (lots of phone calls to identify and resolve the problem), valuing the portfolios (a scarily subjective exercise), researching and presenting ideas, and writing client reports. Such omniscience would be frowned upon today – there needs to be a 'segregation of duties' – but 30 years ago that was the way things were done. My working day was both intense and long; my boss would leave for home around 8pm and I didn't feel I could leave before him. I would pack up soon after and walk home, stopping by the same shop every evening to pick up that sad little bagel for supper. I was almost too tired to eat even that.

On Wednesdays my boss left the office at 4.30pm to go to a church service. I loved Wednesdays!

I was young with no family responsibilities, living on my own in a big city. I could devote myself to the job. But, as I've mentioned, the workload took its toll on my physical and mental well-being. At one point, I took on an extra set of duties: the head of the office (my boss's boss) decided that I would be the ideal person to water his plants and keep an eye on his apart-ment when he left the city for the summer. It wasn't a huge deal in itself, but there was a burglar alarm to negotiate, letters to sort through and plants to nurture over the month he was away. I found it nerve-wracking. What if I didn't set the alarm properly and he was burgled? What if the plants all died? What if I arrived and there was someone in his apartment? My col-leagues told me I was ridiculous to agree to do it; I thought I had no choice.

The exploitation of junior staff today

Despite that early experience, I'm still shocked when I hear about young interns or junior staff working 16-hour-plus days, including at weekends. After speaking at an event to encourage women to consider a career in fund management I found myself walking to the tube station with one of the young attendees. It was 8.30pm. We struck up a conversation and the woman (barely out of her teens) explained that she was heading back to the office. I pressed her on this. It would be nine o'clock by the time she got there, hadn't she finished for the day? She explained that she was doing a summer internship at an investment bank and was expected to stay until 1am every night and to return by 9am the next morning. I asked what would happen if she didn't go back to the office; she had committed to returning to be allowed to attend the event in the first place. Suddenly, she opened up about how hellish she was finding it, how ill she felt – and how trapped. Needless to say, this bright, hard-working young woman was considering alternative careers.

Even if these internships are well paid (and many are not), this is tantamount to slave labour. A 2021 'Working Conditions Survey' revealed that junior bankers at Goldman Sachs average 95-hour weeks and just five hours sleep a night. In the week the survey was conducted, respondents had worked an *average* of 108 hours – which translates as 9am to midnight, Monday to Sunday (plus three extra hours). One analyst said, 'The sleep deprivation, the treatment by senior bankers, the mental and physical stress . . . I've been through foster care and this is arguably worse.' 'This is beyond the level of "hard-working", this is inhumane, abuse,' said another. Such practices are seen as a rite of passage in some organisations, something everyone goes through when starting out, before earning a big salary and putting others through similar torture. Yet the same companies often parade grandiose 'values' and commitments to employees' well-being. Working hard is something we expect to do to succeed, but the volume and pace must – at a minimum – be bearable. I now know I should have pointed out to my New York boss that I barely had the time or peace of mind to sleep or eat. I might have been too nervous to raise it directly, but I could have enlisted the help of a colleague. I probably would have performed better working shorter hours (although my week only averaged a slovenly 80 hours) and taking better care of myself. I certainly couldn't have kept it up for decades. Careers are marathons not sprints, with multiple twists and turns along the way. We need energy and stamina to last the course.

I'm afraid I haven't always heeded my own advice, however. There have been times much further along in my career when I have taken on too much and then only had myself to blame. At the peak of my efforts with the 30% Club I had a demanding full-time job and a still-young family. (Bea was born the year before the 30% Club took off.) I would spend the weekends working on the campaign, feeling guilty that I wasn't spending enough time with the children, before launching into another hard week at work already depleted. Things go wrong when we are too tired to make sound judgements. It became a vicious spiral that I escaped only when things got to breaking point. At that stage I stepped back from 'extra-curricular' efforts, and focused on recovering my mental and physical health and the essentials, including being there for my family. It didn't mean the 30% Club campaign that I cared about so much had to stop: I passed the baton to a wonderful and willing member of the steering committee, Brenda Trenowden, who led the efforts for the next five years.

Work–life balance comes with the word 'no'

Today, with lots of family commitments and no single boss but several demanding part-time jobs, I'm often asked how I balance it all. 'Balance' implies that everything is in beautiful equilibrium. In reality, my life is more of a juggling act. That's a fairly universal experience for 'working' mothers (all mothers work, of course, we just describe those who have paid jobs this way). I've learned to spot the signs of overload, when I'm about to drop multiple balls. Dr Emma Hepburn is a clinical psychologist and author of *A Toolkit for Modern Life: 53 Ways to Look After Your Mind*. She reminds us that we all have a limited amount of capacity and suggests that we think in terms of space in our 'capacity cup': the closer we get to the top, 'the more we risk overflowing with feelings of being overwhelmed, stressed, anxious and exhausted'. As she says, 'recognising that you're near your limit means you can take action'. My signs of being at or near my limit are both physical and emotional. My eyes become twitchy and watery. My energy levels slump. I feel overwhelmed and full of self-doubt. Minor anxieties become irrational fears. At night, I lie awake worrying. Whatever your own symptoms of overload, the signs might be clear but it's hard to stop when that endless list of tasks is mounting. My husband is great at telling me to – no, *making* me – take a break. If you need tough love in such situations, line up someone to give it to you.

Sometimes the causes of overload are things that we can't control – a family crisis, for example. But for 'everyday' (and ideally before I've used up all my capacity) I have finally learned to use that powerful word 'no' when yet another request comes in. It doesn't matter how interesting an offer it might be, if there's no time or energy left, our choice is to either stop doing something else or just say no. Many of us struggle to say no, especially when we are trying to please a boss or colleagues, but ultimately if we don't take care of ourselves, we won't be much good to anyone. It's not selfish, it's sensible. People might be disappointed if they want you to do something, but if it's going to push you beyond your limit, *the answer has to be no*. Today, there's far greater understanding about the importance of good mental health, including at work. There's also a welcome generational shift around talking about it. Younger talent tends to more readily say when it's all getting too much. This is a good development!

Meetings: effective decision-making or time wasted?

In an office environment, it's important to carve out enough time to actually work. That might sound odd but I've been in organisations (both corporate and political) where everyone seems to spend the entire day in meetings and only start doing real work after office hours. Some of those meetings are just about other meetings (!) and they tend to involve far too many people for any proper discussion or good decision-making. And they are often run hopelessly. Just a fifth of managers have ever been trained in the art of effective meeting management, according to Steven Rogelberg, a professor at the University of North Carolina at Charlotte, who's spent decades researching workplace meetings. He suggests that between 30 and 40 per cent of the time spent in meetings isn't productive, nearly three-quarters of us say we do other work in meetings, 90 per cent admit to daydreaming and nearly two-thirds say that meetings keep them from their actual work.[36] I'm sure that none of this is a surprise.

In a 2019 email to employees, Tesla's Elon Musk set out three simple rules for better meetings, along the following lines:

1. No large meetings. He suggests a maximum of six people, but in my experience an able chair can manage up to ten. Larger meetings are really more 'show-and-tell': they might be useful for communicating developments but not as decision-making forums.

2. If a meeting's not useful or you're not adding value, leave. That might sound rude, but Musk suggests, 'It is not rude to leave. It is rude to make someone stay and waste their time.' (Permission to leave has to come from the top with a clear message: improve productivity by not wasting time in unnecessary meetings.)

3. No habitual meetings. Meetings that are put in the diary to sort out an issue often stay there long after it's been resolved. You should only meet when you actually need to.

I'll add a fourth: keep them short. A meeting will expand to fill the time allotted: if you schedule an hour that's how long it'll take, whereas 45, or, better still, 30 minutes will keep the contributions snappier and the focus sharper. People should come to meetings prepared so that the key questions can be debated. Anything needing a much longer discussion can be taken off-line. Issues that need hours of thought and deep research shouldn't be tackled in a single broad-based meeting – a series of shorter ones will keep energy levels high and build towards the solution. If a complex problem needs to be tackled urgently, hold a brainstorming workshop (or 'hackathon') to make it clear that it needs to be interactive – people switch off or lose their sense of accountability unless they are participating. (On that note, consider banning phones at in-person meetings to avoid distractions.)

These suggestions might sound radical if you work in a big corporation with large set-piece meetings. Those meetings might create a sense of achievement, but talking among ourselves isn't necessarily productive. If you're a manager, consider sweeping the whole edifice away and replacing it with more energetic small ad hoc gatherings with a clearer purpose. This is even more important for online meetings where it is harder to get everyone to be unambiguously present. Even if you have many years of practical experience in managing meetings, take training; the best course I ever attended taught me how to chair meetings more inclusively – and with clearer purpose. As someone who had 'learned on the job' there were many things that I had never even thought about before – and which I'm now looking forward to implementing as I take on a role as the chairwoman of a FTSE 250 company. Board meetings are usually long, with many complex issues put to the directors. Given what's at stake (the oversight of a company) it's critical that the discussions aren't just going through the motions. Any meeting can drift right from the beginning, so the chair needs to ensure that the agenda is highly compelling and reflects the purpose of the meeting. The only people who should attend are those necessary to the conversations. The meeting papers should clearly set out the issues and asks of those present and the chair needs to guide the discussion so that it's focused on the points needing to be debated or clarified before decisions can be made. Importantly, he or she must draw out the opinions of quieter members of the group and not let louder voices dominate. The meeting should conclude with a set of actions – with names and dates against them. Many meetings end up just rehashing what everyone already knows beforehand. Good meetings catalyse new ideas, create solutions and move the business on. Otherwise, what is the point?

If you're in a more junior role and finding you're attending futile meetings, raise this politely with your manager and suggest alternative ways of brainstorming and communicating. A good manager will listen to constructive ideas. They may not have realised that the meetings were so pointless.

Time management creates efficiency and minimises stress

Managing our precious time well is critical to success over the longer term. There will always be work needing to be done and there will only ever be a certain number of hours in the day. It's easy to succumb to the pressure to work 'just' another hour or two. But my success at Newton wasn't dependent on long hours worked at the same desk; it was about making the right judgements. That involved prioritising what was important, creating space to listen to others, to think properly and, ultimately, to have the courage of my convictions.

That might sound lofty, but it really boiled down to the more basic matter of time management, as well as learning how to keep my energy levels up. After becoming a mother, I had to be more disciplined. I couldn't just drift towards the completion of a task and leave the office whenever I managed to finish it. It surprised me at first that so much could be done in a shorter time. Mothers (and some fathers) tend to become very good at time management through necessity: the baby needs feeding, the children need a bath and bedtime story and they won't wait for a report to be finished or another email sent. A family makes potentially unlimited demands on parents' time – prioritisation begins at home.

Over the years, my family became reliant on a large whiteboard setting out the day's schedule. I would start writing it early in the morning, using a big marker pen to jot down what everyone was doing and when, whether they needed any special kit and who was collecting or bringing whom. It was just one day at a time – that was plenty. I would often get things wrong at my first attempt and the children and Richard would amend the board until it was (usually) right by the time everyone left for school. When we had a nanny, wonderful Paula who was with us for over 20 years, she would arrive and glance first at the board and then discuss anything unusual with Richard or me. It was a simple device that helped us to manage a potentially complicated life.

I take a similar approach to my working day. A single page-at-a-view diary, with notes in the margins (yes, I still keep a paper version to consolidate different online diaries), and a to-do list that I write at the start of each day. That list used to make me feel rather despondent. Every time I crossed something off, something new needed adding on (sometimes several things). To have a fighting chance, I now prioritise according to import-ance, time-sensitivity and difficulty. That last one needs a bit of explaining: if a task looks likely to be all-consuming, I do a few easy things first before giving the big project my full attention. I've always had an irrational dislike of phone calls, so I get those out of the way early in the day. More positively, I can concentrate for long periods at a time so I will blank out several hours for a major piece of work. You alone know how you work best, so try to create a structure for your typical day that draws upon your strengths and deals with your weaknesses. Unforeseen develop-ments will inevitably throw some days off-course, but if the basic routine is tailored to your life and preferred ways of working, you'll be using your time effectively.

The one-day-at-a-time approach keeps us focused on the present, but it has its limitations. Good time management also involves thinking ahead. When our children were young I created Excel spreadsheets for the school holidays so that I didn't get in a muddle and arrange two camps for the same child in the same week or leave one without any of their siblings to play with. And our family holidays could never be spontaneous with so many people involved (and tastes to please). Filling in the 'advance passenger information' for flights (let alone passenger locator and Covid test forms) is still a dreaded task.

For work, I have a simple 'looking out over the horizon' routine. Every Friday, I go through the following week's diary to get my bearings around what's coming up and make sure I've allowed enough time to prepare for key events. I literally schedule 'prepare for talk' – if I don't, the time will be swiped for something else or I'll fritter it away. Creating the space ensures I have time to think. I've worked with many government ministers over the years and I am often struck by how little space and time they have for thinking. Their diary is fully allocated – even time in a car or on a plane is scheduled for calls or briefings. They are constantly being moved on to their next appointment and, as a result, meetings can feel breathless. In contrast, I once had a boss who drove his diary assistants mad because whenever he got into an interesting conversation, he just let it run its course. It was a refreshing approach, and eventually his assistants learned to put gaps between his appointments. We may have had fewer opportunities to meet him but the quality of our discussions was high.

The need for flexibility in the workplace

Of course, we can only manage our time properly if we have a degree of control over how we spend it. 'Cracking the Code', a 2014 study by business psychologists YSC for the 30% Club, set out to identify practical enablers for women's career success.[37] The researchers took various theories and tested them against the reality. They considered, for example, whether formal flexible working arrangements eased women's path to the top. It turned out that very few senior women they surveyed had ever had such arrangements; instead, they'd benefited from *informal* flexibility – being trusted to work in an autonomous, agile way. At the time, formalised flexible working was more likely to be perceived as being granted a favour and as such an obstacle to promotion.

This chimes with my own experience: I've never had a formal flexible working arrangement but I was given a large degree of latitude over my time even when quite junior at Newton. This was highly unusual in the 1990s. My visionary boss repeatedly told me that if I needed to leave early for a family matter he completely understood. He even pointed out that women's haircuts usually took much longer than men's! (Male colleagues would often pop to the local barber's at lunchtime.) His comments were supportive, not patronising. Female friends in senior roles confirm they've also benefited from 'unofficial' flexibility, helping them to focus on what's important. We've all experienced the jibes that come with such self-direction: 'leaving so soon?' 'nice of you to show up', 'taking a half day?' But if we deliver results, meet deadlines and proudly *own* our autonomy, those voices eventually quieten down.

Such jibes will hopefully become a thing of the past, since the pandemic exposed the truth: being physically present isn't a requirement for producing great work. A shift towards *flexibility as the norm* is long overdue in a digital age. It doesn't just help women and families; it opens up more career opportunities to those living outside major cities. And, as we covered in the last chapter, there are benefits for companies too: the revolution in working practices can be a win-win.

As more of us get to organise our time around what really needs doing, we must remember to consider our own health. We need to take care of both mind and body, finding time to exercise, to eat well and to switch off and unwind. A common trait of successful people is a high level of energy – working out how to sustain yours is a good investment.

Enjoy exercise that is right for you

In my usual way, I struggled for years to find the right form of exercise. I tried lunchtime aerobics and step classes (I'm too uncoordinated to keep up), swimming (too much hassle drying my hair), a personal trainer (too expensive and nerve-wracking) and yoga (enjoyable but sometimes too New Age). I'm hard to please! Eventually, after having my youngest child and feeling self-conscious about my terrible posture (I was lopsided with a badly stooped back), I tried reformer Pilates, where the exercises involve resistance. It was just right for my body, the classes were convenient, challenging but manageable, and it was reasonably priced (four classes for the same cost as one personal training session). A decade later I still love it and can see and feel the benefits – I feel stronger, more flexible and (somewhat) toned. Actress Isabelle Adjani accurately describes Pilates as 'pure torture during the session, but I come out feeling light on my feet and clear in my mind'. I missed the 'torture' during lockdown. We tried outdoor Pilates classes together as a family with an online instructor: fun, free, but less of a regime. Long walks and cycle rides with Buddy running along beside us became our exercise of choice. There is some form of exercise that is just right for you, and it's worth persevering until you find what that is. I was over 40 when I discovered what works for me! It will build your stamina, boost your self-esteem and energy levels and help you stay healthy – including maintaining a healthy weight.

The weighty problem of discrimination

Weight is a fraught and sensitive topic for so many women, along with our often-complex relationships with food. I have shared my experiences of anorexia. Most of the research focuses on the career implications of being significantly overweight, but it's not great to be extremely thin either. Psychologist Stuart Flint of Sheffield Hallam University led a study, 'You're Not Hired!' where participants were asked to evaluate candidates for different jobs on the basis of hypothetical CVs with photographs showing people of varying weights, including very thin, overweight and obese (with a body mass index of over 30). Men and women of 'normal' weight were judged most employable, with obese women least suitable.[38] Other studies confirm that obese people are less likely to be seen as 'leadership material' and more likely to be expected to work longer hours for lower pay than other colleagues. Upasna Bhadhal, 36, runs her own business, Kaleido, which helps firms connect with diverse talent. Upi has struggled with being overweight her 'entire life'. A year and a half into her first job in the City, she embarked on a drastic diet, losing over 20kg (3 stone) in three months. She dropped from a UK size 14 to size 8. She initially felt empowered, that she could wear anything she wanted, and although she knew that she was good at her job, the 'final piece' was in place: her looks. The results bore that out, 'I went from doing well to being one of the most successful people in the company. Clients and colleagues responded quite differently to me, the way people looked at me and talked to me completely changed. People who had known me for years and never paid me any attention were now very attentive.'

The evidence is clear: obese people are discriminated against because of their weight. Weight is not a protected characteristic;

there are no laws against such discrimination unless a person's obesity is deemed a disability.

We know that perceptions matter, even if it would seem fairer if they didn't. Assumptions are often made that overweight people are lazy or lack discipline even though there are far more varied explanations for their size including ailments such as lymphoedema, a chronic swelling, usually of limbs, due to a poorly functioning lymphatic system. They also might simply be happy the way they are. Given the risk of girls 'growing up absorbing the eating anxieties around them' (Susie Orbach, author of the seminal *Fat is a Feminist Issue*), 'body positivity' is a welcome movement, encouraging self-confidence whatever our body shape. Candice Huffine (UK size 16–18), now 36, recalls 'marching to New York [aged 15] in my jean shorts and a tank top to get a contract. I think about that girl all the time, because she didn't let any outside influences change her. I was very surprised when I was met with a lot of rejection.'[39] The fashion industry has, finally, woken up to the risk of showing 'size zero' runway models and now uses models of various sizes, although truly 'plus size' remains a rarity. The beautiful British model Alva Claire, a 'mid-size' 14–16, who's walked for Versace and Rihanna's lingerie label Savage X Fenty, says, 'I feel radical in this industry just by being here.'[40] She and other 'curvy' models are showing us what we already know: that there are many ways to be beautiful. I've mentioned the ground-breaking advertisements for Dove soap, showing women in all their differing natural beauty. The manufacturers, Unilever, dropped the word 'normal' on over 200 products after a 10,000-person study across nine countries, including Brazil, China, Nigeria, Saudi Arabia and the United States, showed that seven out of ten people felt that the description had negative effects. Eight out of ten of those aged 18–35 felt that the word 'normal' could make people feel excluded.[41]

None of us should feel pressured to fit a narrow beauty stereotype. But when our weight interferes with our health – as mine has done in the past – it's time to take action. It's a secondary issue, but that's also likely to be the point when it's most impacting our career.

Healthy body, healthy mind

I Don't Know How She Does It author, Allison Pearson, wrote a piece in lockdown entitled 'I need to lose weight – and so do you, Britain', referring to the 63 per cent of British adults who are overweight or obese.[42] She acknowledged that it can be awkward to talk about, but it's important that we do: obesity has played 'a tragically large role in the death toll from Covid-19'. As the British Prime Minister admitted, being 'way overweight' was a major factor in his own brush with death. That's not fat shaming, it's recognising the health risks. Having changed her diet, Allison says that she can 'now see my toes again. It's a start.' Small steps soon add up to a big move forward; the most important thing is to take that first step.

We want to feel well, not just to look well. Taking care of our bodies also helps our mental health. Exercise boosts our self-esteem, helps us to sleep better and to concentrate. A healthy diet with limited alcohol, sugar and caffeine fuels our brain as well as other organs. But a healthy mind requires more than good food. We need strong and positive relationships, a feeling of self-worth, a sense of purpose, stable routines, support networks and time to explore our interests and ideas, as well as the space to relax and to sleep well. The pandemic undermined so many of those basic building blocks for good mental health that it's hardly surprising that anxieties and disputes became magnified, with a surge in divorce applications and calls to domestic-abuse and mental health helplines.* More than 42 per cent of people surveyed by the US Census Bureau in December 2020 reported symptoms of anxiety or depression, up from just 11 per cent the year before. Young people have been particularly badly affected, worried about their futures and missing their friends – but no one has escaped unscathed. There are people who are terribly lonely, others trapped in an abusive relationship, many afraid about their financial situation. Even if we are among the luckier ones, it's easy to feel despondent.

At the same time our more stripped-back lives during the pandemic reminded us what we really value. During the first lockdown, my eldest daughter and her young family returned from California to stay with us. Our household then numbered 13. While the juggling act became frenetic, it was a precious time with our grandchildren, the weather was glorious and we felt optimistic that our loss of freedom was temporary. That optimism proved unjustified, but the experience showed me that I had been too busy before, and that happiness and fulfilment lie much closer to home. My family was among the fortunate ones in having this reset moment together. Fathers who had never worked a day from home in their lives before told me that they were enjoying family dinners (and lunches and breakfasts) during the week for the first time in *years* and had suddenly realised that so much of their working life had been spent doing things that were unnecessary and unimportant. They determined to do things differently post-pandemic and to live a healthier, more grounded

---

* Stewarts law firm reported a 122 per cent increase in divorce enquiries between June and October 2020; Refuge, the charity behind the 24-hour national domestic abuse helpline reported a 61 per cent increase in calls in the year to March 2021 and in November 2020 mental health charity Mind warned of a 'second pandemic' with more people in mental health crisis than ever recorded and soaring helpline calls.

life. Business travel, a seemingly compulsory feature of many executives' lives, takes its toll, both physically and mentally: I've gone to Boston for an afternoon, Australia for two days. Now we've seen the light, it's unlikely that we'll ever return to the same pace and frequency of international trips – good news for both our health and the environment.

Helping ourselves and others cope with mental setbacks

Many of us feel that our mental health is generally good, but there are times when we struggle. I'm often asked how I cope with setbacks. As Oscar Wilde put it in *The Picture of Dorian Gray*, 'experience [is] merely the name men gave to their mistakes'. We're much more likely to be able to deal with such 'experiences' when we're starting from a good place, generally centred, positive about life and feeling supported. But we all have wobbles; the key is to stop a slight or temporary decline descending into an abyss. One of my children has OCD tendencies. When the repetitive behaviour starts, my husband and I know to intervene, drawing our teenager away from a potential spiral of anxiety with sport, conversation, Bible studies and fun family activities. Other situations will require quite different responses. A friend of mine is currently traumatised after suffering domestic abuse. She just called me about a new development, which she says, 'sounds so small, but I really can't deal with it'. She's on the edge because of the bigger issues in her life. I'm trying to help her see that the new problem is minor but the big one needs urgent resolution. We need to watch out for friends, colleagues and family whose bandwidth is reduced and to proactively support them. Warning signs of mental illness include paranoia or disproportionate anxiety, long-lasting sadness, a tendency to be easily irritated, severe mood swings, withdrawal, difficulty in concentrating, disorganised speech, heart palpitations, chronic tiredness and dramatic changes in eating or sleeping habits. It can be harder to spot when we are physically distanced, but you might know someone who's normally outgoing and now barely talks, or another who seems to be struggling to finish even basic tasks. If in doubt, pick up the phone. Ask how they're doing, listen and offer your support. Encourage them to seek professional help. If you have the opportunity, take Mental Health First Aid training so you can learn how to recognise and help someone who's experiencing a mental health issue and escalate it. Reasonably priced courses are available online and in person through social enterprise Mental Health First Aid England (www.mhfaengland.org) or your employer may sponsor you to take a course. We reach out to our friends because we care, but acts of kindness are also good for us: one of the Mental Health Foundation's top ten tips for looking after our own mental health is to help others.[43] We'll feel needed and valued, and it will also help us to see things from another person's perspective.

The worst thing anyone can ever say to me is 'I know you're too busy.' That really hits a nerve. I *am* busy, but some things are obviously far more important than the next item on my to-do list. And there is no such thing as too busy when it comes to supporting a friend in need. In a world where there's still far too much violence, harassment and discrimination, women have a special responsibility to help each other – and to ask the many good men in our lives to look out for us too.

Takeaways from Chapter 8

1. A common trait of successful people is a sustained high level of energy; working out how to maximise yours over the long term is a good investment. Sleeping well, eating well, exercising regularly, having a sense of purpose and good relationships are all important elements of your physical and mental health and stamina.

2. Internships and junior-level roles can be over-demanding; try to find a way to ask for better working conditions if you are in a permanent state of exhaustion (it's best to seek allies rather than going straight to the top). Work hard but work well.

3. If you have a tendency to take on too much, line up someone to give you 'tough love' and tell you to stop or at least take breaks. When we are very tired, things tend to go wrong.

4. There will be difficult moments when you can't follow your routine – try to go easy on yourself at those times.

5. Managing our weight so that we feel healthy is an important aspect of building stamina. If we're very overweight or underweight, we're in danger of not performing as well as we could. We might be perceived less positively, too. This doesn't mean going on an extreme diet, it means taking action step by step to regain our health.

6. There is a form of physical exercise that will work for you – including fitting in with your other time commitments. You might just need to experiment to find out what it is.

7. Mental health problems have been increasing. Learn to spot the signs of worsening mental health in both yourself and others – and reach out if you sense someone might need

support. Encourage them to seek professional help – and do the same if you are struggling.

8. Helping friends and colleagues boosts our own mental well-being.

9. The pandemic has reminded us what we truly value – and what we have missed. This can be a reset opportunity to ensure that we focus on what's important in the future.

Chapter 9

The Great Taboo: Women's Health and Life Experiences – How to Deal with Women's Issues When it Comes to Work

'When new moms first come back to work they need someone to tell them, "You are going to feel crazy. It's OK to feel crazy. You won't always feel crazy."'

Overheard at 'She Runs It'
Working Mother of the Year Awards 2017

Over 80 per cent of British adult women will have children by the age of 45. Around one in seven women has fertility issues. One in eight known pregnancies ends in miscarriage. We might have very painful, debilitating periods. We will all go through the major life change that is the menopause, and the perimenopause before that. Our hormones, physiology and health issues differ from men's. Yet career guidance for women is, once again, generally lacking in advice on how to deal with all of this. As a result, most of us suffer in silence or feel anxious about how to handle certain situations. My most traumatic experience in the office was suffering a painful miscarriage when I was 12 weeks' pregnant. My goal that day (besides just keeping it together) was to make sure that my colleagues were completely unaware of my physical and emotional turmoil. As the boss, I felt extra pressure to carry on as if nothing was happening, even though I had extraordinarily heavy bleeding and was in floods of tears every time I could escape from my desk and hide in the loo.

I wish I hadn't been so stoical now. We're human beings, not machines. A 'stiff upper lip' perpetuates the myth that strong, capable women simply 'keep calm and carry on'. I'm convinced that the need for pretence is one reason why many brilliant women give up, feeling discouraged and isolated. They're not weak to pause or abandon their careers when going through a difficult pregnancy or struggling to cope with sleepless nights, they're rational – and honest. It's heart-breaking that we don't compare notes more often. Women have told me time and again that they feel they are the only one who can't 'do it all'. That's an expression I have come to loath. Every time I'm held up as an example of a woman having it all (or worse, 'superwoman'), I want to shout, 'You should see me most of the time!' I am very grateful for my life, but the reality is far less glossy than it's portrayed. Yet we hold back from telling it as it is for fear of being judged and being seen as not quite up to the job. It's time to come out as human beings and show that real strength comes from acknowledging and accepting that we're not perfect, that our lives aren't perfect, that we do have setbacks and problems but that doesn't make us any less good at our jobs.

The unspoken private life

It's not just women who feel the need to put on an act: men keep secrets, too. Business in the Community's 'Equal Lives' report published in 2019 revealed that while women are eight times more likely than men to be the primary care-giver of children, they are only one and a half times more likely to be the carer of adults, often elderly parents. Nearly two-thirds of working men who care for an adult haven't disclosed this to their employer. As one man said, 'I started in a new role just before my mother became dependent. I haven't been honest, as I don't want to be labelled flaky in my new team.' Too many of us find ourselves in a state of constant contradiction at work: we are thinking one thing but feel we need to *say* something quite different. That is very stressful. Nearly 60 per cent of the men who are secret carers said they were thinking of leaving their job because of the stress of their double life.

My young friend in banking sets out a better way to do things. One of her parents was very ill and she was struggling to deal with the situation. Initially, she tried carrying on as usual at work, figuring that she needed to show a degree of toughness – not least because she was the only woman in her team. But one day she decided that she really needed to tell her boss what was going on, even if it meant showing a more vulnerable side. She hadn't anticipated his reaction: he was very supportive and immediately appreciated that, at that particular moment, work wasn't the most important thing in her life. She has since been more courageous both about showing her vulnerabilities and asking for technical help from more senior colleagues. Two years later, she says that opening up has definitely had a positive impact on her career; she has a wider network and a broader range of supportive colleagues than the men in her team, who she describes as afraid to ask for help.

Her network includes very few women, however, especially at a more senior level, and she finds that disheartening since she can't really see her next step. And it concerns her that the women seem to leave once they start having a family, usually in their thirties. The very few who are left typically don't have children, which leaves her with few people to ask advice from as she looks ahead. She says the subject is 'completely taboo'.

It's lunacy that we don't talk about something that's such a big part of so many of our lives. Women would feel far more confident about their career prospects with a family if the topic were more openly discussed. There are exceptions: Newton's head of HR invited me to lunch *before* I joined the company and he made a point of telling me that the firm offered a generous maternity package before adding that *I didn't need to work there for two years to be eligible.* I was 27 years old, married with a two-year-old son at the time. I was being told *it's OK to have another baby.* I was very surprised – and relieved. It was such a contrast to my previous company, which only offered the minimum statutory maternity pay (at the time, six weeks at 90 per cent of salary and up to another 12 weeks at a flat rate of about £100 a week, which barely covered the cost of nappies) after a minimum of two years' full-time employment.

What can you expect as a new mother?

Unsurprisingly given my large family and career in the City, I'm often asked for advice from young women thinking of having children, pregnant women or those experiencing motherhood for the first time. I'm delighted to speak candidly and to share both my experiences and what I've seen work for others, including those who've had their children more recently. My aim is to equip the women who approach me with the knowledge and reassurance to be able to focus on what's important at any one moment in their rapidly changing lives rather than living in a constant state of anxiety about what might lie ahead. In particular, there are things that they can do to be more in control of how they are perceived and treated so that their career continues advancing alongside their family, if that is what they want.

When someone contacts me, I'll tailor my suggestions to their specific situation, but there are consistent themes:

1. Take things one step at a time A young woman once approached me. She and her boyfriend had just got engaged. They were thinking of waiting a couple of years before getting married and then two or three years after that before having children. She had just been offered a promotion. Should she take it? (This is a true story.) *Yes!* I (almost) shouted. Whatever your future plans, keep going in your career as the opportunities arise – unless those opportunities really are incompatible with your plans (for example, an overseas posting that wouldn't involve your partner). For a start, life does not always unfold in the way that we hope. It might take several years before a baby arrives, or something might happen that means you become the breadwinner. Or you might simply discover that you find work fulfilling and change your mind about staying at home for very long. Whatever you do, do not 'leave before you leave'. As Facebook's COO Sheryl Sandberg says, 'Keep your foot on the gas pedal until your life actually changes. Then you can make the decision to keep driving quickly, slow down or step out of the car.'

2. Think carefully about when and how you announce your pregnancy

Every time I was pregnant, I worried about how to tell my boss, when to tell him (it was always a man) and what my colleagues would say. By the time I announced I was expecting my *ninth* child, they were entitled to make a few jokes. But I found it difficult to share the news even about my first, second and third pregnancies. With hindsight, I should have made it clear to my first boss from the minute I told him that I remained very committed to my career. The second and third times I just couldn't work out the right moment, so I wore baggier and baggier clothing until I'm sure it was completely obvious to everyone. By the seventh I think I cracked it! My boss was based in Boston. I decided I needed to tell him face to face (always best, if possible). We were both attending a company offsite in Florida. We arranged a breakfast meeting, and this was my chance. He seemed in a cheerful mood, the sun was shining, the food was delicious. I told him I had some news, that I was expecting another baby. He offered his hearty congratulations, but I could see from his expression that he was worried. I pointed out that I was 'only' going from six to seven children, not from nought to seven. I'd done this many times before. His face brightened. 'Yes!' he said, happy again. 'It's only a 16.7 per cent increase.' I laughed – and so did he.

I was lucky. I know one guy who completely disapproved of any woman having a child (not conjecture – he told me so) and tried to have any pregnant women transferred from his team (in the end he was the one who had to leave). If you have a bad experience, *tell someone*, ideally a senior female colleague who you trust (the formal guidance is usually to go to HR; in my experience, however, it's best to get an ally onside first, especially if you are in a junior role). The law is on our side (but could be improved) – we also need to use it. Don't just assume it will all be fine. If you need further help, contact www.pregnantthenscrewed.com, a charity working to 'end the motherhood penalty', set up by Joeli Brearley, who was sacked two days after telling her employer that she was pregnant with her first child. Joeli's experience is not the norm, but sadly it's also far from unique. Prepare for the best, and if things turn out differently, take action.

3. If you're eager to further your career with a baby, spell out your ambition before going on maternity leave. Two colleagues at Newton did this brilliantly. One, aged 40 when she had her first child, and with a key role in the business, asked me for 'maternity mentoring' during her pregnancy. As her due date approached she told me in a very clear, determined voice, 'Helena, I've been waiting so long to have a baby, and I really want to enjoy my time as a new mother. I'd like to work part-time in the first year after my maternity leave, but I don't want you to think this is because I'm any less ambitious or committed. I love doing the strategic projects, I want to continue building my career, but at first, I want to balance my time a little differently.' Her message was perfect and I told her so. Companies can't ask a pregnant woman what their plans are, or how ambitious they are, so *spell it out*. Don't leave a gap to be filled with (the wrong) assumptions.

The other colleague went even further. We had been thinking about transferring another fund to her to manage, a highly visible increase in responsibilities. She was heavily pregnant and her (male) manager's first, reasonable, thought was that we should wait until she got back from maternity leave before moving the fund. She came to see me and argued strongly that she should be handed the portfolio straight away so that she could make some changes before going on leave. She realised that there might be some publicity about her taking over the fund when her due date was so close – that was fine by her, too. We talked about her longer-term ambitions; she was very clear that she had a lot more to offer. We moved the fund across to her straight away. Both women have since had their second children and their careers have flourished.

4. Find a 'maternity buddy' We introduced this at Newton, pairing up a woman who was expecting her first child with a colleague who'd gone through the whole experience recently. It wasn't compulsory of course, but most pregnant women took it up and said it was really helpful to have someone to confide in. I didn't officially have a maternity buddy, but I was expecting my first baby at the same time as the most senior woman in the company. (Our babies were actually born on the same day.) Up until that point, we had barely spoken – she was ten years older than me and I was a little afraid of her. When we were pregnant, she would pop up to my floor in the evenings. Usually we were the only ones in the office by then (something I now realise says a lot about us). We'd switch into expectant-mother mode, discussing everything from how we were feeling to whether it was OK to drink coffee. I was struck by the serendipity of our 'twin' pregnancies. I was the first of my friends to have children and would have had very little opportunity to chat about it otherwise. If your firm doesn't offer a maternity buddy programme, either suggest it or ask someone to step into that role for you – she'll probably be delighted.

5. Try to enjoy your new and ever-changing shape Long gone are the days of frilly, fussy tent-like maternity dresses – thank goodness. Why should we suddenly want to wear a giant white-collared floral pinafore just because we're pregnant? These days you needn't even adapt your style (much). Go to your usual favoured brands and see if they offer a maternity range or clothes 'that you can wear while growing a human' (Reformation). J. Crew, the preppy American label, designates a section of its website to 'maternity friendly' items, mixing up regular clothes-that-work-with-a-bump with specially tailored pieces. If your normal style is floaty, you have an advantage. If you would rather go for proper maternity styles (and they can be the most comfortable, especially for the later stages), there's a wide range of well-priced maternity workwear options on the high street. Seraphine, JoJo Maman Bébé and eco-friendly Isabella Oliver are popular specialist labels. I lived in a brown wraparound dress from Isabella Oliver when expecting my seventh; it was almost the only outfit other than a voluminous jersey trouser suit that worked with the combination of an August due date and swollen legs. Tights and boots were just weird and far too hot at the height of summer but that dress was long enough to cover most of me while the block colour made it suitable for work. A wraparound wouldn't be my usual choice, but it meant that I could style the dress differently, with various tops or necklaces. It's rarely worth indulging in designer pieces: you can upgrade basic maternity wear with wonderful accessories, or rent or borrow for special occasions. To be honest, I could hardly bear to look at my maternity clothes once my baby was born. For a start, I was bored of them; at a certain point in pregnancy you wear the same clothes in rotation (for what feels like) *forever*. Maternity jeans came out again for my subsequent pregnancies, but that was about it. There will be days when you feel like an elephant and have *nothing to wear* that feels comfortable, let alone suitable for work. Find a fail-safe outfit that you can count on for those days. Getting dressed should not be an added stress for pregnant working women, although it often is. Ask your friends for their suggestions and advice (they may also be happy to lend you items). After the baby's born, you may well not snap back into your previous shape, so try to be patient. I often rushed to be slim again, but it was healthier for me and the baby when I took everything more slowly.

6. (But really the number-one priority) **look after yourself and your child** Some women sail through pregnancy glowing throughout. Others – like me – feel sick the entire nine months. Your health and the baby's health tie as the top priority. Don't suddenly take up running or feel pressured into throwing yourself into a new project to 'prove yourself' at work. If you feel good, say yes, but don't stretch yourself to breaking point. One of the wonderful things about taking time out from work for the very special reason of having a baby is the perspective it bestows: you see that 'urgent' task as just something that needs to get done, not the most important thing in the world.

7. **Stay in touch with work, but first enjoy time with your new baby** Over the first two weeks after having a baby you should not work (this is actually specified in the UK's statutory maternity leave law. Interestingly, it's four weeks if you work in a factory). I had to break those rules occasionally; for example, when Millie arrived a month early and I hadn't completed my handover notes. But time with a newborn is incredibly precious. It can also be exhausting! Preserve your energy and focus for your baby. I was really not up to doing anything beyond caring for myself and my family for at least the first six weeks. But later, make the most of keep-in-touch days that most firms offer so that you feel less daunted when the time comes to return to work – and are visible, from time to time. If you can, avoid being completely 'out of sight, out of mind'.

8. **Plan your return to work carefully** The amount of maternity or shared parental leave you take is a very personal decision,

influenced by many factors including finances, health (both yours and your child's), emotional well-being, a partner's desire to also take leave, your access to childcare and, of course, your career. You won't know exactly how you'll feel, so don't fix your plans too soon or in concrete. I'm often asked, 'how much maternity leave should I take?' but there is no right answer. Since I had so many children, taking a year each time would not have worked as far as either my career or family finances were concerned. If you have two children in three years, being away for more time than you are at work inevitably pauses your career – although it doesn't mean that you can't accelerate again later. A year or two really isn't a long time in a multi-decade career. But I went back to work far too soon after having Millie (just seven weeks). I was anxious about the funds I was still responsible for, and both Richard and I felt that it would be better to return to resolve things, but I wasn't ready and those first few months felt like climbing Mount Everest (or at least how I imagine that would feel). These days, fathers have the option to take shared parental leave, giving men the opportunity to spend time with their baby *and* change the assumptions that might cause employers to be wary of hiring women of childbearing age. Most companies don't offer equivalent financial benefits to fathers, however, so many couples make a pragmatic decision for the mother to take all the leave.

Irrespective of how much time you take, be aware that it might feel strange when you first return to work. I felt as if I was having an 'out of body' experience every time I came back after maternity leave. For a start, as a new mother you get accustomed to having a small body attached or close by. If you return to work when your child is a year old this might be less of an issue, but it's still quite disconcerting to be by yourself again. This is another of those closely guarded 'secrets'. Meanwhile we feel pressured (often by ourselves) to sweep back into the office, wearing pre-pregnancy clothes, looking as if we're ready for anything. I tried so hard to look 'she's back!' and again I wish I had been more honest. That glossy exterior disguised a lot of inner turmoil. We want our colleagues to think that we can handle everything, but we can still be human about it, showing that we're glad to return but not picking up as if nothing has happened since we were last in the office. The times when I got it right (my last three babies), I phased my return – working two or three days the first few weeks, then four days for another month or so – or mixing up days in the office with working from home. (The new hybrid ways of working will make it easier for returning mothers to come to such an arrangement.) I could give my all on the days I was in the office, knowing that I would be recharging and back with my baby the following day. Whatever plan you make, remember that it's quite an adjustment and you might feel quite different from how you expected to feel. Adapt the plan if it's not working. Our eldest son went to a day nursery close by my office at first. This seemed sensible and realistic given our budget, but every time he sneezed they called me to take him home. We had to work out a better arrangement. As you find what works for you, try to maintain some perspective. A few weeks' delay or part-time work will not affect your long-term career prospects, but collapsing or feeling constantly miserable or stressed just might.

Planning your return

If you're still breastfeeding and expressing milk once you are back in the office, there are many physical considerations. I have expressed milk for all my nine children and have a bizarre level of expertise about breast pumps, storage, sterilising units, and so on. But no amount of experience could spare my blushes if a meeting overran and the breast milk started to flow. If you have a long meeting to sit through, have your pumping kit ready in your bag and excuse yourself. Always wear pads to stop the first drops coming through – and this is a good time to wear jackets even if that's not your usual style. My worst experience was arriving to speak at a conference in Monaco when my baby was just seven weeks old. I was still on maternity leave and really should not have been pressured to go – and even then, I should have said no. The journey was long and the final stage was in a helicopter, which obviously didn't have nursing facilities. I was already supposed to be on stage when I arrived, and the gentleman who came to escort me wasn't picking up on my hints that I *really* needed to go to the bathroom. In the end, knowing it would be painful in every sense to go on stage without expressing first, I just leapt into a ladies' loo, leaving the guy having to wait for me outside. My stage appearance was even more delayed but the audience would have remembered me rather strangely if I hadn't made that detour.

Planning your return to work includes having a proper discussion with your manager about their expectations, any changes that have occurred in your absence, and generally ensuring that you have the opportunity to contribute at a pace that is realistic. If you're not sure at this point what you want out of that first phase back at work, let the boss do most of the talking. If, on the other hand, you're desperate to get back and be given lots of challenging work, speak up. I've heard of mismatches in both directions: returners who feel they're not being given interesting assignments *and* those trying to ease their way back in being asked to write major reports in the first week. (That's unfair *and* poor business practice; if someone has been away for a year, they will need time to get back up to speed.) Ask for training if you have missed anything critical. Speak up if you are being set unrealistic goals *or* not stretched enough. And always remember, a few weeks or even months in a multi-decade career should not make any difference.

Finally, *remember that nothing lasts forever – and when times are tough cut yourself some slack.* This was my mother's wise counsel when I was at a point of meltdown. There are times in life that feel hard. Combining a very young family with a full-time career is quite likely to be one of them. My entire early 2000s were a blur. When I became a CEO in 2001 I had five children and the youngest three were born in 1998, 1999 and 2000. I'm not looking for sympathy; my family was clearly a choice, and although the unexpected promotion was a great opportunity I didn't have to take it. But it *was* a great opportunity, perhaps a once-in-a-career chance. I took it even though the timing wasn't ideal, and I worked as hard as I could both at my job and at home. Yet I often felt inadequate, not quite good enough whatever I was doing or wherever I was. There was no way to press pause on one big part of my life while I focused on the other. I felt guilty, too – something I've come to appreciate is inevitable for mothers, whether we work outside the home or not. But the children were happy and healthy, the business was thriving and now I can see I was overly harsh on myself. Women tend to be self-critical: we work incredibly hard and achieve a lot and yet beat ourselves up for the things that we can't do. Now at the end of each day I try to take a moment to reflect on what's been achieved and how much I have to be thankful for. It's a much better approach than dwelling on whatever hasn't got done or the unresolved problems.

My mother was right: things pass. Children really do grow up quickly, making it extra-important to enjoy their early years as much as we can, despite the challenges. The issues change rather than disappear as they get older, of course, but those tiny babies and small toddlers who were so dependent become thoughtful, interesting children, teenagers and then adults who contribute so much. Each family is different, with its own demands and dynamic. I have several friends and colleagues with disabled children who have decided to job-share or take occasional sabbaticals, depending on the nature of their child's disability and their work. Increasingly, companies are offering support groups for parents of disabled children, single parents, new parents or just parents. If yours doesn't, why not set one up? (Just make sure you share the load of any organisational burden.)

Motherhood and employers' perceptions

I hope this helps; however, things don't always go as they should. In the 21st century, we should not be worrying as much as we do about the impact having children might have on our careers. After all, most *couples* have children and most parents – men and women – work. Parenthood is the norm, not an exception, and it should be a wonderful experience. As my own life shows, it's perfectly possible to forge ahead with a career while also playing a big role in family life. But as you also know, I missed out on a promotion when I first had a child. That was a long time ago, but the evidence suggests that we need to stay alert to the risks.

In 2015 the Equality and Human Rights Commission (EHRC) looked into the extent of pregnancy discrimination.[44] Such discrimination is illegal in the UK under the Equality Act 2010, but it still happens. The researchers interviewed both mothers and employers. More than three-quarters of mothers said that they had a negative or discriminatory experience during pregnancy, while on maternity leave or when they returned to work. Half said that maternity had adversely affected their job security, status or opportunities for promotion, interesting work or training. One in five had experienced negative comments about their pregnancy and a similar proportion said that they had missed out financially because they didn't get an expected promotion, salary rise or bonus. Ten per cent of mothers said their employer discouraged them from attending antenatal appointments. And 11 per cent said that they felt forced to leave their job, including 1 per cent who were dismissed, 1 per cent who were made redundant and 9 per cent who were treated so badly that they felt they had to leave.

All this makes for grim reading.

The employers' almost universal declarations of support for pregnant women and those on maternity leave were hard to reconcile with mothers' adverse experiences, so in 2018, the EHRC probed employers further.[45] Their anonymised responses were quite revealing:

- Nearly half (46 per cent) of employers think that it's reasonable to ask women if they have young children during the recruitment process.
- Thirty-six per cent of private-sector employers think that it's reasonable to ask women about their plans to have children in the future during recruitment (although it's illegal to do so).
- Fifty-nine per cent think that a woman should have to disclose whether she is pregnant during the recruitment process.
- Forty-four per cent of employers agree that women should work for an organisation for at least a year before deciding to have children.
- One-third believe that women who become pregnant and new mothers are 'generally less interested in career progression' when compared to other employees.

- Forty-one per cent believe that pregnancy puts 'an unnecessary cost burden' on a company.
- Fifty-one per cent agree that there is sometimes resentment among employees towards women who are pregnant or on maternity leave.
- Around a third (36 per cent) of employers disagree that it is easy to protect expectant or new mothers from discrimination in the workplace.

You might be shocked by these revelations. But knowledge is power. No one would say now what was said to me 30 years ago, 'there's some doubt over your commitment with a baby', but they just might think it. I don't want you to be worried about the statistics but to be aware and remember how important it is to manage perceptions. When you are at the point or close to the time of starting a family, it's natural to be highly sensitive about the implications for your personal and professional life. Inevitably, there's a lot of uncertainty. But you're not going to lose your skills, intelligence, competence, talents or experience. You might not feel brilliant when you are pregnant (at times, I could barely spend ten minutes at my desk due to acute 'morning' sickness – which, in my case, lasted all day), but like my former colleagues, you can signal that you remain very much interested in career progression whenever you get the chance. (Create those chances if they don't naturally occur. Ask for time with your manager.) I've mentioned the importance of allies before: confide in someone more senior than you, who's 'been there, done that' and who will champion you. And if you decide that it's right to take a few 'gap years' when your children are young, today this is perfectly compatible with returning to a meaningful role later. There are many returnship programmes to help you – look up www.womenreturners.com or www.reallyhelpfulclub.com for advice on how to get back to work after a break.

The positives!

The good news is that once we make it through the childbearing and early years stage, senior women leaders 'see it as a pit stop in a Grand Prix' according to the 'Cracking the Code' report. Nearly a quarter of those interviewed describe the *positive* effects of having a family on their careers, including the benefits of having a broader perspective, enhanced personal and organisational skills, being more empathetic and more determined to succeed. I'm often asked by journalists (no doubt looking for an attention-grabbing headline) whether having lots of children helped me to become a better people-manager at work. I'm always careful not to talk along the lines of 'the children at home are easier to manage than the ones at work' but there are certainly parallels.

I will never forget the precise moment when I suddenly realised that even though I could relax in my career when Richard found a well-paid job, I really didn't want to. We had two children by then and I had overcome so many hurdles that I wanted to build on what I'd achieved, not give up just as my career was really starting to take off: for myself, for the family and also because I could see other women taking heart from seeing that it was perfectly possible to emerge 'on the other side' with children and continue to progress at work.

Women's issues – don't bear them alone

Of course, pregnancy is just one of many 'women's issues' that might affect us. Sadly, I know women who have had fertility problems or multiple miscarriages; terrible experiences that affect them in many different ways. You'll hear about Jenny

Halpern Prince's struggle with infertility in Chapter 11. She wanted me to include it so that women going through a similar experience could read her story and take comfort. I've noticed a heart-warming pattern: women who have made it through these challenges want to help others going through them. If you are struggling to conceive – or experiencing repeated miscarriages – you might well not want to share widely with colleagues but I suggest you tell one of those valuable allies or your boss. Soon after I experienced that awful miscarriage in the office, a colleague very sadly lost her first baby at 22 weeks. Hers was a truly terrible loss; when she was ready, we talked – emotionally – about it; while I felt helpless in the face of her sorrow, as her boss I could at least show her how sorry I was, that I understood something of what she was going through, and emphasise how important it was that she looked after herself physically and emotionally, rather than worry about work.

Even everyday life has its challenges. Whenever I'm talking to any large group of young women, roughly a quarter will be on their period. I don't know a single woman who never suffers from cramps, headaches or worse. We carry on regardless unless the pain becomes completely debilitating, but that means once again we are putting on a performance for at least part of the month.

And then we go through the perimenopause – which many of us hadn't even heard about until recently – and the menopause. There is now far less mystery about the whole experience and more information available, but this is a relatively new development. Jenny Halpern Prince is candid about her own experiences. Like many women, Jenny was taken aback by the onset of the perimenopause, when we can have inexplicable mood swings, hot flushes and in her case, very heavy bleeding. She recounts being at a meeting with an important client and suddenly realising what was happening, having to escape to the bathroom and work out an exit strategy. Jenny was subsequently diagnosed with endometrial hyperplasia, catalysed by hormonal changes (and treatable). She's keen that we talk more – including with other women at work – both because we'd understand better what is happening to our bodies *and* we'd feel less alone. As Jenny points out, whenever she has reached out to female friends and colleagues about her difficult gynaecological experiences, it's transpired that they are widely shared.

I'm now going through the menopause. My own 'change' has coincided with the issue becoming more openly discussed and with less embarrassment, but also with the pandemic *and* a new phase in my career. *Everything* has been changing and after many years of 'success', I suddenly felt as if everything was going wrong. That might sound melodramatic but that's really how I was feeling. Initially I tried to 'soldier on', but found it very hard to function properly after my sleep was frequently disturbed by a combination of night sweats and heightened anxiety levels. As someone who's had plenty of interrupted nights after so many babies I thought I'd manage – but I was wrong. A quick Google search led me to a doctor specialising in 'bioidentical' HRT: the treatment helped enormously.

Friends suffering extreme hot flushes during the day have changed how they dress to accommodate the sudden changes in body temperature: thin layers are ideal. And one took HRT solely because she was experiencing 'brain fog', another common symptom which can obviously impact our ability to perform well at work. In her case, HRT made a big and very welcome difference. Again, my philosophy is simple: don't suffer in silence and don't suffer unnecessarily.

The physical changes are manageable, but we should also talk more about the psychological impacts of the menopause. For a start, as Jenny puts it, 'it's so unsexy'. There's nothing glamorous about the symptoms (though we certainly don't miss periods). But there's also an emotional hoop to jump through: the menopause closes a chapter on both our ability to have children and the time when we are conventionally considered most attractive. As the mother of so many, you might think I'd be totally relieved to have my childbearing years behind me. In fact, the opposite is true. It's a wrench, knowing that something that has brought me so much joy is no longer possible. Being the mother of young children has been a big part of my identity for a long time: for two decades, I had children aged three or under. I can completely understand why Jools Oliver, 'proud mum of five' and Jamie Oliver's wife, said she was 'pining' for a sixth child before her 47th birthday. Neither of us, I'm sure, would suggest that our 'loss' is in any way comparable to a woman who desires children and reaches the end of her fertility without having them, but there is still an acceptance process to go through. This phase in our lives often coincides with ageing parents, teenage children going through their own hormonal changes – *and* significant responsibilities at work. *Not* being open and honest – and supportive of each other – seems the more problematic route, for both employers and ourselves. Let's keep sharing ideas about how to deal with this tricky time, including how to alleviate symptoms that might affect us at work. Having dealt with the physical side through HRT, I've gradually let go of wistful thoughts about the loss of my youth by consciously turning my attention to the future, to the next chapter, and what I can make of it.

Which brings us to the final frontier, ageing not just gracefully but with impact. Those of us who've made it through to senior levels in our career have the opportunity and a responsibility to help younger women, as well as each other. We can help the next generation over the remaining hurdles while continuing to work to remove those hurdles. To do that we need to have impact. The good news is that middle-aged women are no longer consigned to being 'invisible' – it's a time to use your experience well and be the person you want to be.

Takeaways from Chapter 9

1. Most couples have children. It's the norm, not the exception. Yet we are still far too tentative in addressing this reality in the workplace. Maternity feels a 'big deal' when it comes to women's careers.

2. It's therefore natural to be concerned about possible impacts on your career, but there are steps you can take to be more confident. The immediate aim is to be able to concentrate on and enjoy the next stage rather than being in a constant state of anxiety about what might happen later on.

3. Take charge of sharing your news of pregnancy and be clear about your level of ambition (ideally signal this before you go on maternity leave so that false assumptions aren't made in your absence) – and keep being proactive as your experiences unfold.

4. Find a 'maternity mentor' or 'buddy': anyone who is willing to share their experiences and who is a few years ahead of you. Ideally find a champion, too: someone who watches out for you, is more senior and powerful and can be both a sounding board and an advocate.

5. Enjoy spending time with your newborn baby. Later (when you're ready), use keep-in-touch days to stay visible and involved.

→

6. There is no 'right' amount of maternity leave (just as there's no 'right time' to have a baby). It's a very personal decision. Whenever you return, be prepared for a slightly disconcerting experience at first. Seek to manage your health first, since that will help you in your career more than rushing in before you're really ready. Remember, a few weeks or months won't make much difference in a multi-decade career.

7. Pregnancy discrimination does happen, even though it's illegal. The law is not perfect, but it is on our side. Speak to someone you trust if you have a bad experience – ideally a senior female colleague in the first instance (don't necessarily go straight to HR).

8. If you decide to take time out to bring up young children there are increasing opportunities to return to work through specialist organisations such as www.womenreturners.com.

9. Maternity is clearly only one 'health' issue that affects many women. If you are going through fertility problems, struggle with painful periods or the menopause, or have other 'women's health' problems, look for advice and a support network online or through talking to other women. So many of these problems are shared, and yet we suffer in silence and think that we are the only ones who can't cope. We can and must help each other more, and breaking our silence is the first step.

Chapter 10

What's Next? Ageing Well and Paying it Forward – How to Get Better with Age

> 'Ageing is an extraordinary process where you become the person you always should have been.'
>
> *David Bowie, one of the most influential and best-selling musical artists of all time*

When we were in our twenties my husband and I attended the wedding of a university friend who was marrying a much older man. His mother read a lesson during the service. She was the most wonderfully dressed woman I had ever seen and carried off a magnificent hat with ease. I found out afterwards that she was 73. She was as far from being an 'invisible' older woman as it was possible to be. I was inspired. I didn't want to wish my life away, but I vowed to be 'like her' in my seventies.

I'm not quite there yet as far as either age or elegance are concerned, but I'm certainly enjoying feeling more 'the person I should always have been', as the late, great David Bowie described ageing. Hopefully, we enjoy each of our decades for differing reasons: in my fifties, I'm feeling less worried about the wrinkles than I thought I'd be and more appreciative of my ever-changing family (a third grandchild is on the way) and the possibilities that still lie ahead. Those possibilities include spending more time doing what's important to me, helping other women to succeed through championing and mentoring individuals while working to remove the remaining barriers for women's general progression. I'm conscious and very grateful that my influence has increased with age, which is not something I'd expected and is not something everyone experiences. I feel a responsibility to do something useful with that influence.

I do have lots of unfulfilled ambitions, but again they are not what I might have imagined 20 years ago. I'm determined not to retire from the City until it's more inclusive and caters better to women as customers and employees (I may never retire!) and of course I want my family and friends to be happy and healthy. I've stepped off the executive career ladder to take on a portfolio of roles, which gives me more autonomy and the ability to align my work with those remaining ambitions. I have to work harder for less money than before, but that's a trade-off I've chosen. In fact, I've become choosier about a lot of things, and similarly aged friends feel the same way, even if some restrictions remain: time, finances and health. We're less worried these days about 'ruffling feathers'; we've worked out what really matters and we're conscious of the sands of time. Whatever we're doing – and our lives are more diverse than ever, with some of my friends now full-time carers of both children and parents and others still pursuing full-time executive or political careers – we typically don't feel 'past it'. We're not paragons of virtue but we're aware of the benefits of good nutrition and regular exercise, managing stress and generally looking after ourselves and our loved ones.

WHAT'S NEXT? AGEING WELL

Ageing today – a non-issue?

It's a good time to be middle-aged; the *Daily Telegraph*'s 2020 'best dressed' list of 25 women included no one under 40. That seemed a little unfair on many stylish 30-somethings but the point was well made: it can take time to hit our sartorial stride. A 2019 *Vogue* supplement celebrating 'ageless style and beauty' was entitled 'The Non-Issue', proclaiming that 'age should no longer be an issue'. As Edward Enninful, editor-in-chief and mastermind of British *Vogue*'s makeover in recent years, put it, 'Promoting diversity ... has never been solely about a person's ethnicity or gender. It's about diversity across the board. Seeing the amazing array of women over 50 proves that a person's age will always be a more intriguing, nuanced and inspiring factor than a simple number could ever suggest.'

This is very heartening to those of us in that age bracket. There are so many fantastic older style role models who are obviously women of great substance, too. A favourite of mine is Prue Leith, who I once met when we were both speaking at an event to celebrate the Open University's 50th anniversary. She was just as wonderful in person as she is on TV: warm and open, and she was wearing bright-red spectacles that, needless to say, matched her outfit. She's developed her own very recognisable style and keeps ramping it up as she gets older, while her career continues to go from strength to strength. Prue is an incredible 81. Helen Mirren (75) is amazingly glamorous, and no one would think of adding 'for her age'. As she says, 'Age is not the issue ... but how we perceive age is. How we incorporate it and embrace it in our lives. How we treat those older than ourselves.'[46] Iman, David Bowie's beautiful widow, model, actress and entrepreneur, is now 65, another example of someone who looks more gorgeous as the years progress, along with Yasmin Le Bon, a couple of years my senior, a supermodel for three decades who wears her everlasting beauty nonchalantly. Of course, these are all very wealthy women, able to afford beauty treatments and the best nutrition. But we can all take care of ourselves, as we covered in Chapter 8 – being reasonably fit, maintaining our weight at a healthy level and looking after our skin needn't cost a fortune. Some of the best skincare on the market is the reasonably priced Boots No.7 range, for example. Making a small effort every day – including protecting our skin from sun damage – pays big dividends later on. And having a positive mental attitude is one of the keys to avoiding premature, damaging ageing: believing that we can do so many of the same things tomorrow as we did yesterday, only with the added benefit of experience. Seeing ageing as progressing towards becoming that more experienced, wiser, perhaps *kinder* person is an interesting, exciting prospect.

My older role models are certainly all success stories who seem to have grown in confidence with the years. And yet many women feel far from glamorous in their fifties or sixties, let alone their seventies and eighties. They do feel invisible or unhappy about the changes that time has wrought on their appearance. We held a children's party a few years ago, and one child's grandmother came to pick her up. She was very attractive, well dressed and the mother of someone quite famous, yet she seemed to shrink when she entered the room and was surprised when my husband struck up a conversation with her. She was so interesting, and yet her body language suggested that she assumed no one would find her so.

In Chapter 1, I said that even the most 'together' women suffer from moments of self-doubt. Those moments can become more frequent and the feelings more intense as we age and become aware of losing something, even our sense of identity. We have sudden realisations as we look in the mirror or see a photo that we are not the youthful person we picture in our minds. It can be crushing, especially if that realisation coincides with a difficult time in our lives. An 'empty nest' as children leave home, relationship woes (divorce rates are highest for 45- to 49-year-olds), concerns about both elderly parents and children, and medical issues, are common problems but that doesn't make them any easier to bear. It can all start to feel downhill from here. I came across another uplifting quote, from General Douglas MacArthur, American five-star general:

> Youth is not a period of time. It is a state of mind, a result of the will, a quality of the imagination, a victory of courage over timidity, of the taste for adventure over the love of comfort. A man [or woman] doesn't grow old because he has lived a certain number of years. A man grows old when he deserts his ideal. The years may wrinkle his skin, but deserting his ideal wrinkles his soul.

General MacArthur went on to say, 'You will remain young as long as you are open to what is beautiful, good, great . . . '

It's not just a romantic thought. I know many people much older than me, who are or were genuinely young in spirit. Professor A.D. Buckingham, who I knew simply as David, was a distinguished chemistry professor at Pembroke College, Cambridge. When I was at the university, his elder daughter was away studying at Oxford during term time and I rented her bedroom in Professor and Mrs Buckingham's beautiful house. In early 2020, David turned 90 and my husband and I were honoured to be invited to his joyful birthday lunch at Pembroke. I sat next to the 'birthday boy' for part of the meal. He quizzed me with the same enthusiasm as he had over breakfasts in the family home 35 years earlier. We had a wonderful time. Sadly, David died a year later, but his attitude remained youthful to the end.

Our attitude to the outward signs of ageing

Whatever path our life has taken, keeping a positive, inquisitive state of mind is the most important guard against the sadness that can beset us in middle and later years – and it is critical if you are still working. Many women I know who are making a big impact in business and government today are in their fifties, sixties and beyond; they have the benefit of years of experience and remain energetic and enthusiastic. It's a powerful combination.

Yet those outer wrinkles can bother us, too. My own reactions to becoming aware of a fresh sign that I'm physically ageing used to be quite unhealthy (ironically, the signs are coming far more frequently now that I deal with them better). I'd first feel a sense of dismay mixed with denial. Was it because I'd slept badly? Did I have an extra glass of wine that could explain why I looked particularly wrinkly/haggard/saggy/exhausted? Once past the disbelief, I might look up non-surgical treatments. The only one I have actually done (so far) was Exilis Elite on my lower face and neck, a radiofrequency treatment that stimulates collagen pro-duction. I invested in a short course a few months before my son's wedding. I'm not sure it made much of a difference, but it was a psychological boost and the sessions were very relaxing. I'd book them for a Friday late afternoon after work and felt completely chilled and ready for the weekend afterwards. Judy Murray has displayed the 'before' and 'after' results of her own non-surgical facelift 'Morpheus8', which are amazing. I worked with Judy a few years ago on an initiative to encourage more women to play sport; she's such a vigorous personality with a wonderful zest for life that I don't remember her having any wrinkles at all, a reminder that one of the most effective anti-ageing 'treatments' is to smile.

Our skin and hair changes along with our hormones, and with the passage of time. I've changed my skincare regime in the past couple of years, which seems to have helped at least slow the deterioration and, most importantly, I've become more accepting. Those wrinkles and imperfections are testament to my life so far, a life that I am grateful for, including the setbacks and difficult times. My skin and body have been through a lot, including many wonderful experiences, even if they have caused some 'damage' and although I occasionally have a wistful moment wondering if it might be possible to turn back the clock on parts of my body, those moments quickly pass. Would I ever have 'tweakments'? I hope not. I hope I'll stay happy enough in my own skin to pass up anything more than a glorified facial. I did have Botox once – and it made my forehead very smooth – but my eyelids (already hooded) became droopier. It was as if the signs of ageing had just shuffled down my face. I have experimented more successfully with 'Healing Natural Oils', American products that incorporate homeopathic ingredients and natural essential oils. The company has an extensive range – I've used the product designed to get rid of ugly skin tags that had gradually appeared on my torso. It worked!

Like many of my contemporaries, I've yet to come to terms with the ageing process as far as my hair is concerned. My mother had almost black hair and went completely grey in her twenties; my original hair colour was lighter and it's been a slower, more gradual process. Until the pandemic, I was blissfully unaware of the true colour of my hair, thanks to six-weekly touch-ups. The first lockdown was announced just *before* one of my regular appointments, so my natural colour was revealed all too quickly – a dull half-grey–half-brown that really is the definition of mousy. I resorted to semi-permanent home-colouring tints – Josh Wood and Christophe Robin were both recommended – but the first turned my hair a brownish pink to start with (to be fair, the instructions clearly warned that the product was unsuitable for covering greys) and the latter was too dark and ashy. Lockdown two was shorter, and by that point I think most of us realised that our hair wasn't the most important thing. I was lucky as lockdown three came about – this time I had just visited the hairdresser's, and in light of my previous home-colouring experiences, I decided just to touch up the parting line after every wash with Wella 'Insta Recharge', like eye shadow for hair. The whole experience has made me think about when and how I should go grey. I'm in no hurry but I reckon that by the time I'm 60, brown hair might look rather odd with my face. I came across an article by Kate Spicer, 51, who lived by 'dye until you die' since her first grey hairs at 29 but decided to embrace her natural colour over lockdown. She recounted the experience honestly, pointing out that the first months are the hardest, people are baffled by her decision, that in fact she is still using dye to pep up her natural grey and that the result (which pictures show to be very distinguished) made her think more about how to age in a way that was neither high maintenance nor incredibly expensive but still made her feel good.

We can energise our style as we age

With so much help and artifice available, reaching each ageing milestone has become a personal and financial decision. My ambivalence and hesitancy to fully embrace the ageing process is normal. It's hard to let go of a certain image we have of ourselves.

I remember trying on a skirt in a store and asking another shopper for her opinion, 'Is it too young for me?' She replied rather ominously, 'Well you'll never be this young again!' (I bought the skirt, figuring I would enjoy it for as long as I could. It now hangs in a daughter's wardrobe.) But I have realised – especially since starting an Instagram 'career dressing' account – that this is a time when it can be fun and energising to turn up the volume on our style rather than retreating into the background. I started the account because I was being asked so many questions by women about what they should wear to work. I had left my full-time job and had more freedom and time to post what I was wearing each day. That was November 2019. I started tentatively, in a Zara dress (I was nervous about wearing anything expensive) and at first, posted twice a day, showing my (few) followers where my dress had been that day. As I grew more confident and less concerned about negative comments (Instagram is a much more positive community than Twitter), I brought out my designer dresses alongside high street pieces, upped my style game and featured an eclectic mix of friends, colleagues and daughters on Fridays. Once we started working remotely, the posts shifted to a mix of working-from-home advice and 'dress-up' rather than 'dress-down' Fridays, involving ball gowns in the garden – just for fun, really. I can now tell in advance which posts will be most popular (I analysed 2020's posts, one every weekday, so it's not just a hunch): the spectacular gowns are most 'liked' and also attract the largest number of comments, followed by uplifting colour, family moments and, finally, posts where I show vulnerability – for example, a make-up tutorial that started with my naked face. Buddy is a regular companion in the shots and has a very dedicated following of his own. I've retitled the account 'dresses and thoughts for the day' – the photographs are really a springboard for my reflections – and I love the camaraderie that comes through the conversations. A wonderful group of women is very actively engaged and I really look forward to hearing their opinions and suggestions each day. Some are 'career women', others have stopped – or are yet to start – working, are doing a mix of projects or looking after children or elderly parents. They span a wide age range, from teenagers to octogenarians. We have more in common through our interests in both style and what's going on in the world than anything else. And our lives are inevitably a mix of joyful and sad times (especially over lockdown, when it's been obvious that many are very worried, and missing friends and distant relatives). We seem to pull each other up when that's needed.

The psychological boost of looking our best

I have to confess that there's been another big benefit from the timing of my foray into Instagram: getting dressed and doing my hair and make-up for a photo has motivated me to continue making an effort during both the pandemic and at a time of considerable change in my career. What started as a reflection of my personal style is now helping me to preserve and evolve it. Every weekday I'm reminded that getting properly dressed really can be a psychological boost. I enjoy thinking about what I'm going to wear and say, and it makes me experiment more: to keep coming up with looks I need to pair separates imaginatively and refresh dresses worn before with different shoes, jackets or jewellery. A Friday disco post featuring my very best 'mum dancing' was – to date – my most pushing-out-the-boundaries moment and also the most fun. I did look silly, but I also looked how I felt: happy and less afraid of negative reactions than hoping my 'moves' might make people laugh at the end of a long week in lockdown. (They did!) Nothing ventured, nothing gained.

Passing on our experience to others

The Instagram conversations show how willingly women reach out to share advice and ideas. A benefit of decades of experience is being able to help those who haven't had them yet. Many women aren't formal mentors but help their friends, children and younger colleagues every single day by listening and offering advice. This is a wonderful thing. The older women I most admire are indeed confident and often stylish; they are also very generous and kind. When the 30% Club was just getting off the ground, I contacted many successful British businesswomen, but some were disinclined to help. 'No one ever helped me,' said one. I was both astonished and aghast, replying, 'Wouldn't you have rather that they did?' It was disappointing, although I'm very grateful to the women who thought differently. Today we can see that there's so much more to be gained by helping each other and ensuring that the generation of young women coming up behind us does not encounter the same hurdles that we did. We might not have known how to ask for a pay rise in our twenties or thirties, for example – but we do now. We felt awkward about asking for more money – and so might a young woman today. If that applies to you, prepare for the big ask. Do your research so that you know your value. Refer to your positive performance appraisal. Make sure that you've already signalled your ambition (and asked one of us to put in a good word for you). In other words, go in armed with a strong case. Stick to it. Be factual not emotional, but be gracious about it. Get straight to the point if you worry you'll lose your nerve. And think about how you'll react if the answer is 'no' (there might be a company-wide salary freeze, it might not be personal). And tell your mentors how the conversation went – we will want to either offer further help or celebrate.

The best women actively champion their protégés, leaving little to chance – and they cherish their successes. Meanwhile, there's hopefully much to celebrate in terms of our own progress – and that includes being more able to be ourselves whatever we are doing in later life. The worries about getting it wrong tend to subside as we grow older; we have some perspective about what's really important and trust our judgement more. That includes over what to wear. I'll see a dress (online, usually) and love the neckline and the shape but know it's too short for me now. It's *always* a pass, however much I love those other aspects. A check-list runs through my head. If I'm shopping for a jacket, it needs to be fitted. To have a neckline that suits me. To work with the shirts, skirts and trousers I already own. To give me some structure around the shoulders and curve through my waist and hips. To be a colour that suits. That will leave a very small range of possibilities. In the past, I might have been tempted to buy the least-worst option; now I'll hold out for what really works. And if I order something and it's not quite right, it goes back *immediately*.

We also want to be comfortable. Michelle Obama's head-to-toe burgundy outfit by Sergio Hudson at President Biden's inauguration won many plaudits. It was a great chic look by the emerging designer – wide trousers and polo neck, pulled together with a statement belt and sweeping coat – but it also looked cosy for the January ceremony outdoors in the middle of a pandemic. The former First Lady's stylist, Meredith Koop, said that Michelle Obama told her afterwards, 'I was so comfortable!' She looked and felt fabulous.

Michelle Obama (57) is a very inspiring woman, both for her style and her substance. We love seeing what she wears on the big occasions. She often surprises – her sparkly thigh-high Balenciaga boots teamed with a canary-yellow dress that she wore for an interview with Sarah Jessica Parker (the last stop on her 2018 book tour) are still talked about. Footage shows that she even took care to reveal just how high those boots went up her long legs as she entered the stage. During that interview 'MO' told 'SJP' that during her eight years as First Lady she learned that 'fashion does have meaning'. She knew that her clothes would be dissected, no matter what topic she was talking about. And she decided to make the most of that rather than feel resentful. 'I did know that my clothes were making a statement . . . So we decided why don't we use this platform to uplift some young new designers who normally wouldn't get this kind of attention, because you can change their lives, which is one of the reasons why we chose Jason Wu for my inaugural gown.' She also pointed out that Jason Wu didn't expect it, in contrast to some of the established big designers. 'You learn that there are people in this scene who feel entitled to these things . . . and I hated that feeling. There are a whole lot of people out there who are trying to make it, there are young women and immigrants and black folk.' And finally, 'I didn't want to wear the clothes of someone who didn't have a good spirit . . . and you could hear how they treated my staff or how they treated their workers so everyone I wore as far as I knew had a good spirit as well.'

Michelle Obama was obviously in a very special position of influence as First Lady, but plenty of people have power and don't use it half as wisely. Our own platform is likely to be (considerably) smaller, but if we have *any* opportunity to improve things for the next generation, whether it's by supporting local businesses, helping a young student with few connections find work experience or just listening to the girl next door who's not quite sure what she wants to do with her life, let's take it. And if you're the one needing help (and that includes plenty of older women), pick up the phone and call a friend. Tell them how you are feeling. I'd be surprised if they are not delighted you called and happy to talk.

*

Takeaways from Chapter 10

1. Ageing doesn't need to feel that it's all downhill. In many ways, we become more relaxed, more sure of ourselves, more 'the person we were meant to be'.

2. Hopefully, as we grow older we are able to increasingly focus on what's important to us. Our lives are unlikely to have gone in a straight line. We'll have suffered setbacks, but also have great experience that gives us perspective.

3. It's wonderful to be able to share some of that experience to mentor – or better still, champion – younger women.

4. Ageing is also an opportunity to dial up the style volume rather than becoming invisible.

5. Taking pride in our appearance even as time inflicts unwelcome changes is important for our mental as well as our physical health. Looking after yourself in small ways each day is the surest path to ageing well: use sun protection, take at least a moderate amount of exercise, eat healthily, sleep well and have purpose.

6. 'Tweakments' (including colouring our hair) are a matter of personal choice (and finances). Growing old gracefully doesn't require accepting every wrinkle or grey hair.

7. Social media can help us to build a network, convey our interests and enthusiasms, and encourage and advise each other. Twitter can be confrontational; Instagram and LinkedIn tend to be more supportive communities.

8. There are some great older role models in their seventies and beyond: women who look great and who have very genuine confidence. Read their stories, take heart from their approach. I like to think of myself as *evolving* rather than declining!

Chapter 11

A Style Masterclass with Six Wonderful Women: Showing Us How it's Done

'The only real elegance is in the mind; if you've got that, the rest really comes from it.'

The late Diana Vreeland,
former editor-in-chief, Vogue and
style adviser to Jackie Kennedy

I'm fortunate to know many inspiring women who achieve great things in their lives and do so in fabulous style. Six of these wonderful women agreed to share the influences on their lives, careers and choices, along with their top style tips. They are from all walks of life, and are women who not only exemplify great style but who also do what they can in their own ways to inspire and help others. Their stories are practical masterclasses, lessons in being a woman of substance and style – in very individual ways.

Jenny Halpern Prince

CEO and founder of the public relations firm Halpern and chair of the Lady Garden Foundation, a women's health charity

Jenny exudes *joie de vivre*. Early fifties, tall, slim and glamorous with long blonde hair, she strikes anyone who meets her as totally 'can-do'. Her positivity shines through the confident way that she speaks and dresses: a mix of luxurious leisurewear and colourful blouses with elegant trousers for work. It turns out that Jenny's style has been honed over her entire life. Her father, Sir Ralph Halpern, was CEO of the Burton Group, driving Topshop's early success and acquiring Harvey Nichols in 1985 when Jenny was still a teenager. Jenny's childhood memories include attending glittering boutique openings and her father bringing her back amazing clothes from his overseas business trips.

It's no surprise that by the time she was 16, Jenny was 'immersed in fashion'. She won a place to study history at the London School of Economics but decided against taking it up, inspired by her father's phenomenal success without a degree. Naturally, he disapproved of her decision. A born presenter, energetic and energising, Jenny's first role (aged 19) was press officer at Joseph, the multi-brand luxury fashion store. For a fashionista it was 'like being in fairyland': Joseph stocked Alaïa, Prada and Dolce & Gabbana, and Jenny spent 'almost her entire salary' on beautiful clothes. With no business experience, she approached her job with an entrepreneurial spirit. When film-makers asked to borrow clothes from the store, she came up with a formula to

charge 20 per cent of the retail purchase price per day – and negotiated a 20 per cent cut of the rental fee for herself. With designer
clothes regularly loaned out for four days at a time, her earnings
soared, along with her confidence. At just 23, she decided to set
up her own communications agency 'feeling there was nothing I
couldn't do' even though her father told her not to expect a penny
from him if things went wrong.

An *Evening Standard* article about Jenny's new venture
prompted a call from hair-and-beauty mogul Daniel Hersheson,
who became her first client. By the fourth month she had as many
clients, including Angels Costumes, which supplies costumes for
film, theatre and television. Jenny would stand in their ware-
house, marvelling at the racks and racks of clothes, but was fired
'on the spot' when Angels decided another of her clients presented
a conflict. The business revenue immediately halved. He may
not have been willing to bail her out, but Jenny credits her father
with the more valuable gift of teaching her to take ownership of
problems. Jenny picked herself up, got the business back on track
and 'felt like a gladiator'. Shortly afterwards, when another client
complained that he hadn't seen any results two months into the
contract, she told him 'I am coming to your office *now*.' Despite
the client's protests, she explained that it takes a lot longer than
two months to build a brand and was kept on for another five
years. Almost three decades later, Halpern PR is a communications powerhouse with an impressive client roster.

Alongside Jenny's business success, however, she struggled
to have children, having 12 rounds of IVF over 11 years. Since
giving up on her dream of motherhood was 'not an option' she
kept going by drawing on the resilience learned through her
upbringing and business setbacks. Eventually, Jenny and her
husband embarked on surrogacy and their twin girls were born
in America, followed by a son seven years later. The twins are

school friends of my youngest daughter Bea, which is how Jenny and I really got talking. After her long wait to have a family, Jenny adapted a famously disciplined work schedule. Managing her time well is critical to *finding* the time to be 'a working girl, a wife, a mother, a good friend, a dog owner' – and the chair of a vitally important charity, the Lady Garden Foundation.

Charitable work

In 2011, Jenny's great friend Tamara Beckwith lost her mother, aged 68, to ovarian cancer and asked if she'd help raise money to fund research at the Royal Marsden. Jenny had her own brush with gynaecological cancer at the age of just 20, when a smear test revealed pre-cancerous cells. And so the Lady Garden Foundation was born, a women's health charity that started life by fund-raising for gynaecological cancers and has since broadened its work to encompass women's reproductive health. Jenny is a fabulous chair – I can vouch for this as one of the trustees. She just makes things happen.

The charity itself is a great example of style meeting substance. It deals with a very serious subject, but Jenny and her equally glamorous co-founders know what people enjoy and respond to best. The events are starry and fun while the stories pull on heartstrings. Picture the actress Joan Collins (literally) sharing a stage with cancer specialists and survivors. That's a very powerful combination.

Jenny's style

I asked Jenny if her celebrity friends influence her style and whether she feels the need to adopt the image of the brands she works for. Jenny thinks very carefully about her audience before she decides on an outfit. If she has meetings with two very different clients in the same day, she'll change so that her looks reflect what's important to them. The Lady Garden events involve 'putting on a show', so she'll dress up. Her other charity work is with Access Aspiration, which provides workplaces to young Londoners from disadvantaged backgrounds. When Jenny visits schools her main goal is to be approachable. Thoughtful dressing is key. But even as a fashion chameleon, she is always a glamazon: always feminine, sharing my belief that 'if you're working in a world of men, it's an asset to be female'.

Her style secrets include using My Wardrobe HQ for renting fabulous dresses for big gala events at a fraction of their cost – and for selling on pieces that she no longer wears. (The rental site was the source of Carrie Johnson's beautiful Costarellos wedding dress for her marriage to the Prime Minister.) Like most of us, Jenny wants to dress well without spending too much. She loves it when people ask, 'Where's that great coat from?' and the answer's 'Zara'. Her favourite Zara coat is bright orange. Jenny brings uplifting colour into her day wherever possible; it suits her cheerful personality. ME+EM is a favoured mid-priced brand; the trousers fit her perfectly (we are all on a quest for the perfect trousers) and the separates work well with Jenny's designer label of choice: the ultra-cool Isabel Marant. For eveningwear she recommends Galvin, not mega-expensive, very flattering and great for jumpsuits, a surprising and sexy choice for big events.

Whatever her mood, Jenny's not going to do business with her hair a mess, wearing no make-up, but she takes just a few minutes to get ready and to get on with her day. She loves being blonde and lets her long hair dry naturally before curling it loosely with tongs – 'it takes four minutes'. She's tried it darker ('hated it'), with a fringe ('ditto') and would never wear her hair up ('my ears are too big'). Her go-to make-up brand is Trinny London. In other words, at this stage in her life Jenny just knows what works. Confident that she's looking her best, her low-maintenance beauty routine and assured style lets her focus on the important things: her family, business, charities, friends and health. Jenny epitomises both style and substance, while wearing it all lightly.

Baroness Neville-Rolfe DBE

Member of the House of Lords, former government minister, senior businesswoman and civil servant

The very first thing everyone notices about Lucy (who's in her sixties) is her streak of bright blue hair. In a newspaper interview after being appointed to the House of Lords in 2013 she said, far too modestly, 'It's the only thing I'm known for.' In reality, Lucy is renowned for being both a formidable businesswoman, having been group director of corporate and legal affairs at Tesco *and* a government minister. She's also very lovely, welcoming me warmly to the House of Lords and providing generous insights into its slightly daunting ways of working – and she is the mother of four sons, and grandmother of five granddaughters. But I had no idea how her famous blue streak – often paired with brightly coloured patterned tights – came about.

Lucy explained that while working on a climate-change project for Tesco she saw someone on TV with a 'beautiful purple streak' in her hair. To celebrate the 'green' initiative, Lucy decided to put a green streak in her dark hair and everyone loved it. When she then went out election campaigning for the Conservative Party it became a blue streak and has stayed that way ever since apart from a brief foray into red, for a trip to Asia. I saw Lucy several times during lockdown – both in person at the House of Lords and on Zoom – and was impressed that her blue streak looked as pristine as ever. She had mastered doing it herself when hairdressers were closed.

Buoyed by the positive reception to her distinct hair, Lucy then discovered wonderful Wolford black-and-cream patterned tights, starting another passion for quirky tights. As Lucy explains, both her hair and tights are talking points: people ask her about them and they strike up a conversation, making her more approachable.

Of course, not everyone has the strength of character to deliberately wear 'talking points', but Lucy has always 'been comfortable being different'. She's intellectually curious, happy to challenge, to scrutinise and to think independently. Her eclectic style and imposing presence stem from powerful family influences. One of five children (three sisters and then, finally, a 'longed-for' brother) she grew up on an idyllic farm between Salisbury and Shaftsbury. But when she was eight, her parents ran into financial difficulties and had to sell the farm, although the family was able to stay on in the farmhouse. Her father (who spoke seven languages) went back to university and switched careers, taking a consulting role in Brussels. His resilience showed Lucy that setbacks needn't be a disaster and that it's perfectly possible to change career.

Lucy comes from an academic, artistic and political family. Many generations have been to Somerville College, Oxford, including her mother and three of her own sons. Lucy studied philosophy, politics and economics there and, after toying with the idea of becoming a landscape architect, applied to three organisations: the civil service, Unilever and the Bank of England. Her decision to join the civil service was based on her perception that they treated women well and she'd be able to further her career with a family, whereas she'd need to move 'at the drop of a hat' at a global company like Unilever. The City 'wasn't what it is today', so she was less convinced about a career at the Bank.

Women were well represented in the civil service fast stream when Lucy joined in 1973, but few stayed on after they had children. Lucy moved quickly through the ranks before becoming the youngest woman promoted to a senior civil service role at the age of 33, by which point she was also a mother of two. That promotion led to her doing a seminal piece of work on planning rules at the Ministry for Agriculture, Fisheries and Food (now the Department for Environment, Food and Rural Affairs). In 1992 (now with three children) Lucy had a 'lucky break', being appointed to John Major's policy unit at No 10 Downing Street. She had 'quite a couple of years' working for the Prime Minister. Seven years after her third son was born, Lucy had her fourth. With the election of Tony Blair and the Labour Party in 1997, and many changes across government, Lucy felt it would be difficult to progress much further in the civil service and decided to make the big jump into the private sector. She enjoyed her interview with the impressive CEO of Tesco, Terry Leahy, and was appointed to a senior role at a time of rapid growth for the company. She became company secretary in 2004 and was promoted to the board in 2006 where she served until she retired in January 2013. The other executive board members at the time were all men, with 'unremarkable' backgrounds and educations. They were also all 'hard-nosed, clever and intensely focused'. 'I was a bit different,' she says. 'One of them called me Camilla Parker Bowles. I made my mark by leading the company's defence in three major competition enquiries, in which the company was under severe threat given its scale and success.' Her other tasks included devising a ten-point community plan and dealing with the fallout from foot-and-mouth disease, which closed down the countryside and delayed the General Election in 2001.

Lucy's style

The career change prompted Lucy to 'tidy herself up'. She describes herself as 'a bit of a bluestocking' up to this point, and an HR manager suggested she speak to an image consultant. I quizzed her on what sounds a potentially tricky conversation. Lucy said that Tesco handled it very sensitively, just offering the consultant's services 'should she want them'. Lucy was happy to take the advice. The consultant helped her to stay true to her individual taste while upgrading her look to reflect the importance of her position in the business. Tesco's Florence and Fred (F&F) team designed a properly tailored suit for Lucy to wear to investor conferences, and she quickly learned about the transformative power of good tailoring. The consultant also taught her that it's the *combination* that counts: a decent haircut, appropriate make-up and a simple manicure all work together to enhance the right clothes. The advice had a lasting impact on Lucy's style. I love the way her look is consistently both creative and professional. As she pivoted to more fitted suits, Lucy stopped wearing black and wore more colourful yet more tailored clothes. These days, she often goes shopping with one of her daughters-in-law, who works in fashion, and happily mixes designer and high street labels, including Marks & Spencer.

A new career in politics

Just before Lucy retired from Tesco she received a call (on Christmas Eve) from David Cameron, inviting her to join the House of Lords. The appointments process took months (as did mine) but it didn't take much longer for Lucy to be offered a ministerial post. In the end, she had three ministerial roles and shepherded eight bills through Parliament in just three years. Now she takes every chance she can to help improve the statute book, applying what she's learned over her distinguished career in both public life and business.

That career has exposed Lucy to different leadership styles. She cites the fabled Terry Leahy as having a 'marvellous style of management', which he adjusted according to people's level of need. Able, experienced people were given considerable autonomy while he spent time coaching those who would benefit from it most. This intelligent approach made a big impression on Lucy. Her other role models include Margaret Thatcher (also a Somerville alumnus), for showing it was possible to get to the top irrespective of gender, and her mother; Lucy says, 'I am who I am because of her.' Clever and artistic, Lucy's mother was frustrated to give up work when she married, but later when her husband was in Brussels she ran what was left of the farm alongside bringing up the family. Strong, stylish, charismatic women have inspired Lucy to create her own impact, from the very first moment when people see that blue streak in her hair and the jazzy tights to when she stands up and gives one of her eloquent, brilliant and often forceful speeches. Lucy's style is truly her own.

Kristy McKenzie

Open innovation success manager, Wazoku

I introduced you to Kristy McKenzie before, as someone who's always felt comfortable wearing her hair naturally, even when she was the only one to do so among her black friends. Kristy, now 30, works in the fascinating area of 'open innovation', where businesses go outside their own organisation to source ideas. It's a fascinating and exhilarating area. But when she first left university, Kristy ignored her instincts and joined a traditional Mayfair-based law firm. That was a mistake. In her words, 'in some places you stick out and you feel celebrated, but there are others where you stick out and *don't* feel celebrated!' She soon left to follow her real passions for communication and technology. Kristy loves the youthfulness of tech, where people dress as they want to (as long as they're decent). She chooses what to wear and how to style her hair each day based simply on her mood and the image she wants to project that day.

How did Kristy get to be so self-possessed at such an early stage in her career? Like all our wonderful women, she credits both role models and being encouraged as a child. She grew up in north-west London and was conscious that her mother 'always wanted the best' for her three daughters, seeking out the best state schools and taking care to build her daughters' confidence. Kristy was one of very few black children at her primary school, but she didn't feel that she was treated any differently. There was just one incident that she can recall, when all the girls were having colourful glitter sprayed in their hair for a play. The teacher stopped when she saw Kristy's cornrows and told her that her hair couldn't be sprayed. Her mother simply took out the plaits that evening and the next day Kristy's afro was decorated with glitter just like all the other little girls. Kristy thinks the teacher was simply unfamiliar with black hair and afraid of making a mistake. At her senior school, Kristy was still very much in a minority but there was more diversity; there were other black as well as Asian students, and Kristy tended to hang around them, feeling 'a sense of comfort'. But as we have already learned, Kristy was the only one who wore her hair naturally. It wasn't just her friends who straightened their hair. As she was growing up Kristy noticed there were few black people on TV and none of them wore natural hair.

After the brief false start to her career and her wise decision to 'fail quickly', Kristy was contemplating a leap into working with start-ups when a friend told her about an opportunity to go to Uganda to work with micro enterprises. These are very small businesses, usually with fewer than ten employees, funded by small loans with the potential to create good jobs and to scale up. Kristy always had a desire to make a social impact. She applied and soon found herself on a plane to Uganda. It was an experience that changed her in many more ways than she had expected.

A career turning point

Access to finance in Uganda is limited, making it hard for people to get a loan to buy or build a house, so they gradually expand their homes as they earn more money. Kristy stayed in a very humble dwelling without a single mirror. She decided not to buy one, choosing to embrace her new environment and finding it very liberating living so simply, not even knowing what she looked like. Having previously been 'very put-together', Kristy relaxed her style, going back to basics, walking everywhere in trainers. It wasn't just the more stripped-back lifestyle that was new. When she stepped off the plane, 'I was no longer black. I was just me.' She was suddenly conscious of the impact of living in the UK with the constant reminder 'that I am a minority. When I read magazines, see billboards, watch TV, I am exposed to so many products and services where I do not see my reflection.' For the first time in her adult life, Kristy was living in a country whose population was majority black, 'where the TV shows, the news, the billboards, all the media presenters had black faces. It was amazing. It was truly one of those experiences where you don't realise what you're missing until you experience it. Being there I walked around with a little more confidence, I felt more peace – it's hard to describe exactly how it impacted me, but it did. It felt like I belonged.'

The experience made a lasting impression on Kristy's confidence, presence and style. The work itself elevated her to 'the boss', suddenly managing a team of 17 people, having previously managed just two. She had to think carefully about how she used the shorter time and fewer interactions with each team member, and her leadership style changed along with everything else. At the end of the four-month project, she returned to the UK and decided to focus on innovation. She went to work for The Bakery – which isn't a bread maker but an 'open innovation challenge-led business accelerator'. That meant little to me, but Kristy explained that it involves helping companies solve specific challenges by partnering with start-ups in their network. Kristy's role required her to distil each specific challenge into a brief and put that to a number of start-ups to find a good fit and, ultimately, a solution. She took me through a real-life example. A multi-national consumer goods company had a problem with their famous razor blades being frequently stolen from shops. In an attempt to prevent the thefts, stores were keeping the blades in a cabinet or behind a lock; however, this discouraged customers from making a purchase. Sales were adversely affected. The challenge was to protect the blades without putting people off. One start-up came up with the idea of shoppers scanning a QR code on the store shelf where the blades should have been found, enabling the customer to fulfil the purchase digitally and collect the blades at the checkout. The company trialled it with their own employees before putting it into practice in real stores.

Kristy's style

Whatever the problem, Kristy has to get on with *everyone*. Her job is to bring all the stakeholders together, people of all ages and levels of seniority with different areas of expertise. To do that, she needs to dress in a way that makes her feel confident. One of her confidence-boosters is to paint her nails – it puts a smile on her face. She often paints them bright pink – this was her one 'indulgence', even in Uganda. Whatever the outfit – and Kristy is quite wide-ranging in her tastes, using clothes to express how she's feeling, rather than sticking to a uniform – her polished nails make her feel ready to go. Kristy is happiest when the sun's out, when she wears colourful, bright prints, switching to darker colours in winter. When we have met, Kristy's look has been very chic, sleek and minimalist. She's never been into designer brands, focusing more on a look than a label and happy to buy anything she likes that's been made responsibly. She wears the clothes rather than letting them wear her. These days at Wazoku, Kristy works with a wide range of organisations, helping them solve their strategic challenges by connecting them with over 500,000 'solvers' across the world. Organisations are realising that although they hire great people, there is a world of untapped opportunity, ideas and expertise that sits outside their company. They can progress faster and uncover new perspectives by sourcing from different industries and specialisms. Kristy loves the variety of the issues she deals with, all linked by an open-source approach to finding answers. To someone like me who believes in the importance of diverse thinking to solve complex problems, it's an exciting concept. As Kristy looks further out to the next phase of her career, she'd like to 'own' the problems as a client, helping to source the best ideas and see the longer-term impact on a business.

Just as we were concluding our conversation, Kristy said that she wanted to talk about a challenge she'd been experiencing since lockdown. As a teenager and young adult, she'd been blessed with 'amazing skin' and never worn much make-up – just mascara and perhaps a little concealer and lipstick when she went out. A few years ago, she started developing eczema, then in 2020, stress triggered it all over again – along with mild adult acne. When her skin conditions flare up, both her confidence and her style are affected; tight clothes aggravate the eczema, the treatment cream is sticky, limiting what she can wear, and she feels she needs more make-up. Having taken good skin for granted, it's been an unpleasant surprise as she approached her thirties to suddenly face not one problem but two. It's made her very conscious of the need to manage her mental health – and to appreciate it when her skin is good. From the moment Kristy and I first met, I've been impressed by her maturity as well as her poise. I'll be watching her career closely, confident that she has what it takes to keep progressing in her own beautiful and self-assured way.

Anne O'Leary

CEO, Vodafone Ireland

I first met Anne (who's in her early fifties) at a fabulous event in Dublin, 'Look the Business', hosted by *The Gloss*, a fashion magazine. We were the keynote speakers at a glamorous dinner for over a thousand Irish businesswomen. A few of my friends were there from the phenomenally successful Irish 30% Club, but Anne knew *everyone*, and everyone knew Anne. She was wearing a sky-blue Roksanda dress with big bows on the sleeves, just like one I have in pale pink, and we immediately compared notes on our favourite designers. That evening we were treated to professional hair and make-up, and Anne's blonde curly hair intrigued me: it was so different from conventional 'business' hair.

A couple of years later, we shared the stage again at the 30% Club's global seminar at Dublin Castle. This time Anne was wearing a very distinctive Dolce & Gabbana dress: a simple shape in a memorable black fabric covered with a child's drawings. I started following her on Instagram and realised that as well as being enormously successful in her professional life, an advocate for women and a stylish dresser, Anne is very committed to health and fitness, enjoying daily dips in the sea whatever the weather.

Anne grew up in Cork. She says it's a running Irish joke that people from Cork have a 'privileged nature', but she feels it's true, that her background and upbringing have made it easy for her to connect. As the only girl in her family (with three brothers) she received a lot of attention and was a natural performer, dancing and singing in school musicals. She was also a competitive swimmer from an early age. A teacher encouraged her to join the debating society: 'she insisted I try out' and Anne is very grateful that she did. In her words, she 'steps up' for presentations, rather than being flummoxed by them; a skill that's been very helpful in her career.

The path from telesales to CEO

Anne hadn't thought too much about any career until the day her school leaving certificate results came through, when her mother suggested she should become a nurse. That didn't appeal to Anne so she went to secretarial college instead. Her first role was at Nixdorf Computers and she ended up in telesales, combining her day job with an evening course in marketing at Cork Institute of Technology. Along with an entire generation of young Irish people in the 1980s and 1990s (including my husband), she moved to London in her twenties with her accountant boyfriend and worked in the marketing team at Reuters. Unlike my husband, Anne returned to Ireland three years later, to sell advertising for Golden Pages, Ireland's Yellow Pages. This was Anne's breakthrough role: she became the company's highest-performing sales executive and was approached by Esat Telecom, a fixed-line telephony company. Esat was then bought by British Telecom, and Anne moved to Dublin and ran BT Ireland's fixed-line operations before joining Vodafone. Five years later she became their CEO in Ireland, attributing her rapid rise to an agile approach, high motivation and 'independent streak'. As Anne says, she always wanted to make her own money, pay her own bills and 'buy whatever she liked' at least as far as clothes are concerned.

Anne's style

Anne credits a close teenage friend, Sandra, with inspiring her interest in fashion. As a 16-year-old, Anne earned money by looking after a family of five children at weekends and loved how the clothes she was able to buy made her feel: more confident, more expressive, more herself. During the years when she was travelling around Ireland by car selling ads for Golden Pages, comfort was a big factor. She was also working mainly with men and 'sought to blend in' by wearing Paul Smith trouser suits. Anne reflects even now on the moments 'in a bad meeting' when she would take some comfort from the distinctive wavy striped lining inside her jacket.

She had just turned 40 when she joined Vodafone and immediately noticed that there were more women working there and that they dressed in a more feminine style, wearing dresses rather than the clichéd trouser suits. Anne remembers thinking she should try something different, realising that she wouldn't feel out of place in a dress. The clincher was the ease of a dress for her morning swims – she just needed to bring one item of clothing. She started buying dresses and 'hasn't stopped'! Anne watches out for the sales and invests in a couple of new pieces every season, wearing her favourites for years. Like me, Anne prefers putting a little cardigan over the top of a dress rather than wearing a structured jacket. We also share a lack of curves and a preference for more fitted styles, although Anne buys her dresses one size bigger than she really needs. She is slim and in fabulous shape, but she just feels more comfortable and thinks that she looks better when her clothes aren't tight. This is a great tip; as I've aged I weigh much the same but the weight is distributed rather differently. To put it bluntly, I'm scrawnier on the top half, more rounded below. Anything tight on my lower half exaggerates things. By just switching up a size for clothes that are fitted around the hips, I have convinced myself that I look slim all over.

We discussed Anne's beautiful blonde curly hair, which is entirely natural. She prioritises a good cut and then it is very low maintenance – she needs a style that dries quickly after swimming. Anne is quite clear that she'd rather use a free hour to go for a run or swim than sit in a salon. She wears light make-up that also works with her sporty lifestyle, and although she likes stacking bracelets, she isn't a 'jewellery person' and generally avoids earrings (another wonderful woman who dislikes her ears). She wears heels to give her a little extra lift (she's five feet four inches/1.63m) but steers clear of uncomfortable towering shoes. When it comes to bags, Anne favours quality over quantity, buying a new one every few years from either Loewe or Bottega Veneta. Both Italian brands make wonderful, if pricey, large and long-lasting bags that hold everything Anne needs for the day. Great clothes and the right accessories lift her mood, boost her confidence and reflect her personality.

Having honed a strong personal brand, working from home necessitated some changes. For the longer term, as Anne says, 'working from home is here to stay', for at least part of her week. She's given her dresses a break and invested in lovely blouses, choosing a different top each week for her all-staff online updates. She knows people are waiting to see what she wears, and it keeps up everyone's spirits – and hers – when she puts on something colourful or distinctive. It gets cold sitting in the same spot for long video calls, so she wears a Hanro vest underneath so that her new blouses are in full view rather than obscured by a jacket or cardigan.

It can be tricky dressing for evening events as a senior woman in business: the dreaded 'lounge suit' dress code doesn't help us at all. I tend to wear an upgraded version of my daytime look on those occasions: full-blown eveningwear is too much, but it feels right to make some effort rather than looking as if I've come straight from my desk. Black tie is a little easier, since it definitely calls for dressing up. Anne has a black-tie formula: she loves pulling out all the stops, but stays true to her signature look. In 2018, Anne won Irish *Tatler*'s Woman of the Year Business Award. She wore a second-hand long glittery designer dress ('80 euros') and had her hair and make-up done, knowing that she would be making a speech and being photographed. She doesn't wait for an occasion to buy something she loves, her approach is simply 'see it, like it, buy it'. Anne has the confidence not to choose an event dress based on its price but on whether she'll enjoy wearing it. Before coronavirus, she had plenty of opportunities to wear special dresses and sees glamorous events as moments to 'represent myself and the company'. Anne's trademark fun, feminine style has become part of who she is, and at this point, she feels a responsibility to live up to expectations. Women come up to her and say, 'I can't wait to see what you'll be wearing' or 'Anne, I love that!' She's determined to continue to enjoy fashion and making it work for her. Anne is a woman empowered by her style.

Upasna Bhadhal

CEO and founder of Kaleido, an innovative recruitment platform

Upi and I have worked together for several years on the Diversity Project, where Upi has very generously given her time and expertise in many ways, including compèring our online seminar in 2020 and leading research into the experience of diverse candidates applying to financial services. I knew about Upi's entrepreneurship, that she is wonderfully articulate and always looks polished and distinct, wearing strong colours and favouring puffed sleeves, but I really didn't know much more about her. A few questions one day prompted many discoveries about Upi's career path and challenges – as well as her views on style and substance, and the relationship between the two. It's an inspiring, honest story.

Upi, in her mid-thirties, describes herself as British-Indian. Her family is originally from Sindh. After the partition of British India in 1947, when Sindh became a province of Pakistan, many Sindhi Hindus and Sikhs migrated to India, fearful for their lives. Her great-grandfather was a wealthy nobleman, but, as they fled, the family was forced to leave everything behind. With little in the way of assets and no land, they turned to entrepreneurship as a family and eventually relocated to London. This background continues to be a significant influence on Upi's independent approach to her career. After a degree and masters in politics, a friend suggested she try recruitment, because she's 'such a people person' and before she knew it, she was working at a boutique search firm in the City, the only woman in the team – and one of very few people bringing in any revenue. One day she was 'walking down Old Broad Street in a cobalt-blue "power" coat with a six-figure cheque in my hand to lodge it in the company's bank account. It was the payment for a placement I had made, the transfer of a team. It was my light-bulb moment and I suddenly thought: *I should be doing this for myself!*'

Having made that decision, however, the path ahead was not straightforward. Upi established her own executive recruitment and coaching business in 2012. She was pregnant within a year with her first child and ended up having three children over three

years. The business initially took off, but Upi hadn't the chance
to expand the team before going on maternity leave. She recalls
speaking to a client on the phone just six hours after an emer-
gency C-section 'because it was just me'. Upi candidly says that
she's keenly aware that friends and clients saw her as 'a superwoman', but at that point in her life everything was 'a bit of a
blur' and she felt 'a complete mess'. Her self-esteem issues were
linked to her long-running battle with her weight that we heard
about in Chapter 8. Upi worked hard to lose the weight she'd
gained in her first pregnancy, only to find out that she was pregnant again – and the same thing happened the following year.
During this phase, she scaled down her business and kept in touch
with the industry through her work on the London leadership
team for Ellevate, a network for professional women.

When Upi coaches businesswomen, she asks them to undertake
a 'career audit'. She decided to do an audit of her own life and
business; she has two daughters and a son, and is ethnic minority, but she realised that she was mainly placing white men in
senior financial roles. Those candidates were seen as 'looking the
part' – they fitted the mould of success in a traditional industry.
Upi decided that she should focus on helping women develop their
careers. This includes helping women find a style that works for
them. Upi has seen first hand the correlation between personal
style and career success, and she reminds candidates that their
personal style is 'the way you say who you are before you say a
word'. She agrees that the best approach today is for women to
wear what makes them feel confident and expresses their personality. Things have changed quite considerably even over the
15 years that Upi has been recruiting: at first, she noticed that
everyone wore a 'corporate uniform' in the financial sector, they
'talked the same way, walked the same way – it was just very
homogeneous'. Upi then started working with a broader range

of sectors, including advertising, where more individual styles of dress were the norm. She started adopting that approach for herself, embracing colour, wearing her favourite puffed-shoulder styles – and noticed how it helped to build her own confidence.

That confidence has been fragile, however. The dramatic weight loss we heard about early in Upi's career, and the change in how people treated her based purely on her weight, was unsettling. She didn't like the new level of attention and 'self-sabotaged', eventually putting all the weight back on.

Breaking the cycle

Upi describes the complicated nature of her battle with her weight, 'I have struggled with my fluctuating weight for the best part of 20 years. I still hear echoes of being told by family members, friends and even strangers that I had "such a pretty face" but "if only you lost a little weight". It is so deeply ingrained in me that every time I go to a conference, networking event or party, I scan the room to see if I am the biggest person there. I usually am. It is very "othering" and yet I'm doing it to myself. I even had a former member of Marie Kondo's team help me curate and cleanse my closet in the hope that seeing all my beautiful clothes – which might not fit but bring me joy – would be the catalyst to make me finally overcome my weight struggles.'

A surprising result of lockdown is that it helped Upi to break the vicious cycle of anxiety over her weight and low self-esteem. 'Lockdown may have taken away every civil liberty but, ironically, as someone who has struggled for so long with my physical appearance, it's been liberating for me. Cumulatively gaining more weight with each pregnancy I haven't felt I could really express my personal style since my twenties. One of the silver linings of the pandemic was the freedom it gave me to live my best life in the sanctuary of my own home. I found myself exploring the dresses I had been collecting for that future moment when I might be skinny enough and brave enough to wear them in public. But that small tile on the Zoom screen has given me the wings to explore my style more confidently than ever before. In this new virtual world of work, we're able to create an optimised image of ourselves and what we share of our home (those curated bookshelves, strategically placed photos and artwork), portraying how we want to be seen regardless of the laundry, mess and kids' toys that may lie just out of shot.'

Upi's style

The freedom to be who she wants to be on Zoom has made Upi feel more self-assured and determined in real life. She now sees herself as the successful woman she really is, as a powerful individual who is creating opportunity for many other women and for change where it's needed. She relaunched her business with a focus on connecting firms with diverse talent. Upi recognises that she uses style to empower her, 'when I want to nail a big meeting or I am speaking to thousands of people, I will wear a great dress or sky-high heels that make me feel formidable'. She's also decided to take her weight-loss efforts slowly, to focus on being healthy and maximising her well-being rather than attempting another extreme diet. She hasn't weighed herself in over a year and is determined not to subscribe to the conventional view that she's 'supposed' to be thin, but instead to dress boldly and enjoy herself. Her new approach is working: 'I am still on a journey to overcome my imposter syndrome and the deep-rooted trauma I have from decades of obsessive dieting. It is a slow burner, but I feel more in control than I have ever been before and that's good enough for me. I am enough for me.'

I'm grateful to Upi for sharing her story so candidly and applaud her for what she is doing both for herself and by creating opportunities for others. She is so much more than 'good enough'!

Asahi Pompey

Global head of corporate engagement and president of the Goldman Sachs Foundation

Asahi and I first met over Zoom when we were both panellists at a City conference on diversity. I was immediately struck by her poise and shining confidence – and that we were both wearing bright-yellow shift dresses. She was also a rarity: a black woman at the top of her game at a big American investment bank. How did she get where she did and in such great style?

Asahi, now in her late forties, has a twin brother, three other siblings and a close-knit family; her parents have recently celebrated their fiftieth wedding anniversary. When she was nine years old the family emigrated from Guyana in South America (population 750,000) to Brooklyn, New York. They lived with her aunt – ten people living in a one-bedroom home. Asahi says it was a very happy home with lots of laughter, fun and church – and a big emphasis on education. She has a 'wonderful network of aunts and uncles, and many of them were schoolteachers'. They were insistent that a good education was the key to a better life.

Eventually, Asahi's family moved into a housing project. Her mother got a job as a bookkeeper at what became New York

University and her father got a job at ConEdison as an operator. Asahi attended a poor-performing elementary school, where less than 20 per cent of pupils attained the national average reading age. At this stage as she says, 'One might argue that's not a very likely path to end up as a Goldman Sachs partner.' Middle school (ages 11–13) changed her life. 'If you looked at the children going in the front door it was an integrated school, but white children were placed in higher streams than black children.' One day her teacher told her 'you don't belong in this class' and she was immediately promoted three streams to the top set. Her twin brother stayed in the lower class and their lives diverged. Asahi is very conscious that her life has 'really been marked by exceptional opportunity'. She was admitted to an excellent high school, although it meant leaving the house at 5.30am and taking two buses and a train. She graduated top of her class but assumed that she would go to a local college since her parents couldn't afford to send her to a prestigious university. At this point, another teacher intervened and insisted that she set her sights on one of the top schools in America, arranging to come to her home when her father had finished his late shift to explain why it was so important and how he would help her through the application process. Asahi won a big scholarship to Swarthmore College, although she had to squeeze four years of study into three before the money ran out – and she still graduated top of her class. The final stage in her education was Columbia Law School. Asahi had US$73,000 of debt after her law degree, which 'seemed insurmountable' and she needed to earn as much money as possible to finance herself and help her siblings through college. She joined a leading international law firm, Cleary Gottlieb Steen & Hamilton, which had just won the mandate for Goldman's initial public offering ('IPO', when shares of a private company are issued for public sale to investors for the first time). Asahi decided, 'the pre-eminent law firm has just got the pre-eminent investment bank as a client, I must get on to this IPO!' Others might have propelled her forwards, but Asahi has always set her sights on certain goals.

A resolution to achieve

After a spell with the law firm, including living in Germany where she met and married her husband, she returned to the United States and was hired as the chief US lawyer for *The Economist*. She loved working for the magazine but realised that if she wanted to further her career she needed to move again. She joined the pharmaceuticals company, Pfizer, and signed up to email lists about industry events, which she occasionally attended. Then in January 2006 she received an invitation to an event for lawyers interested in joining Goldman Sachs and put it on her calendar. On the day 'nothing got in my way preventing me from going', so she went downtown to Goldman's Wall Street offices. When she arrived, there were hundreds of people, 'all swapping business cards'. She felt totally unprepared. But a month earlier she had been turned down for a promotion at Pfizer. She sized up the situation at the Goldman's event and decided to *create* an opportunity. She resolved to do two things: she would be the first person to ask a question after the panel discussion, and at the cocktail session she would talk to the two people on the panel whose contributions resonated most. She did those two things, and six weeks later, she got a job offer from Goldman Sachs – the *only* person at the event who got a job offer.

I love that story!

Like every true story, however, life was a little more complicated. While she was interviewing at Goldman, Pfizer suddenly offered her the promotion. She still joined Goldman but found the first few years tough. 'Back when I joined, depending on the day, it felt like new hires were treated like an organ from another body – it takes time to earn trust, and resilience is required. You've got to be comfortable with being knocked down and not take it personally.' She does add that 'it's a much smoother transition for lateral hires in recent years'. Those first few years taught Asahi a lot about having influence without power and needing the courage to speak up when something didn't look right. Sometimes raising her hand paid off, at other times it didn't. After patiently working her way up and years of cultivating key relationships and mentors, she was asked to join the Goldman Sachs partnership and was offered a more public and influential outward-facing role as the president of Goldman Sachs' global philanthropic effort. Asahi had plenty of experience speaking at conferences, but being thrust into the limelight on TV took the scrutiny to a new level about what she said, how she said it and how she looked. The extra attention extended internally too – suddenly colleagues were asking her about the Fitbit she wore, where she liked to shop, her lipstick colour, whether she kept track of what she wore on TV, whether she styled herself. Asahi welcomed the interest, having long believed that women should feel comfortable talking about all sorts of things at work including what to wear.

Asahi's style

Her personal style has evolved with her career. She laughs about her own 'phase of the pantsuit', which seems to be a rite of passage for any woman working in a male-dominated industry – at least until now. At one stage Asahi had a female boss who wore a 'boxy pantsuit'. 'She was who I wanted to be, so I went out and bought four pin-striped pantsuits. We looked like clones for two years.' At that point, Asahi had had enough of being someone else. She 'just wanted to wear a dress' and was encouraged by the positive reaction.

I told you about Asahi's long dreadlocks that were a defining feature of her look right the way through to her appointment as managing director. At that point in her life, she found herself 'boasting to a friend' about how low maintenance she was. Her friend challenged her, 'Are you high maintenance about your work? Are you high maintenance about your children?' Yes, yes ... 'And yet in the one body that you've been given, you're proud to be low maintenance?' The conversation stopped Asahi in her tracks. She started to take more interest in her appearance and presence in the same way that she did in other aspects of her life. The more attention she paid, the more interested she became in fashion and how others perceived her. She thought about the shape of her body – she 'has hips' but also a small waist. She thought about the colours that suited her, that expressed her personality and, ultimately, what worked on TV. And she considered how she came across, how she used gestures when she spoke, how she carried herself and held her shoulders, the intonation and modulation of her voice. And she concluded that all these things could enable her to be better at her job and to be *seen* as better. As she says, 'Men use all the tools they have. I wanted to leverage all my tools. I thought about how to get messages across. The packaging can make the difference between whether a message has wings or flops.'

I asked Asahi if she dresses differently for TV. Yes – she wears solid colour, smaller jewellery and avoids long enveloping sleeves, preferring sleeveless or short-sleeved dresses. Her preferred brands are Adolfo Domínguez and Massimo Dutti, both mid-priced Spanish designers, and French label Tara Jarmon. She looks for interesting detail at the top of her dresses, something with a little edge. She's not afraid to be noticed. Like Mellody

Hobson, in most of the rooms she's in, Asahi's either the only black woman or one of very few, so she already stands out. The idea of restricting her clothes to try to blend in makes no sense to her. Asahi has her own brilliant way of putting it, 'Let me stand out in the power of who I am.' And now as the mother of two boys, aged 10 and 11, she has 'the best, most honest advisers'.

Finally, I asked Asahi if she ever felt like the token black woman. Oh yes, she replied, 'but I've decided to step into it. If this is the moment I'm given opportunities, I can use it to change things, to seize the chance to bring other women, and other women of colour, along.' Her role as president of the Goldman Sachs Foundation gives plenty of scope – and money – to make a difference. Its main philanthropic projects have been 10,000 Women and 10,000 Small Businesses – and the latest, the more ambitious, One Million Black Women, all programmes designed to close opportunity gaps and advance economic opportunity. She laughs when people ask her now if she was 'always philanthropic', given her early financial constraints; today she is certainly using her position and resources to give others a chance as others gave her. Hers is a wonderful story of what can be achieved with both encouragement and determination.

These six wonderful women all champion others. They lead by example, are authentic, successful, confident, resilient and inspirational. They have all suffered setbacks, moments of self-doubt and great opportunities. They make the most of what they have – and in great style.

They are women of style and substance.

Afterword

Building Self-Belief One Day at a Time

'If you're presenting yourself with confidence,
you can pull off pretty much anything.'

*Katy Perry, singer, songwriter
and* American Idol *judge*

I hope you have found this book helpful. As you've seen, there are
very many practical things that you can do to tip the balance in
favour of your success. Nothing we've considered requires instant
mastery, special talent or expense. All that's needed is thought-
fulness, self-awareness and perseverance. Taking regular small
steps in the right direction every day will build your self-belief
and, in turn, you'll gain the confidence and respect of others.
And although everyone faces setbacks, it's how you respond that
determines whether they hold you back or become springboards
to a higher place. You have agency.

Three final reminders:

1. Focus on your strengths and develop them without limit. Be inspired by others, but make the most of what *you* have to offer. Build a strong personal brand that reflects who you are.

2. Self-confidence can be learned just like any other skill. Take those small steps, but gradually push beyond your comfort zone.

3. Help others along the way. Be good to people. Be courageous and authentic.

Now it's over to you!

Notes

---

1 Research: Is A Picture Worth 1,000 Words or 60,000 Words in Marketing? Matthew Dunn, 12 November 2019. The author set out to investigate the oft-quoted claim that people process visuals 60,000 times faster than words, a statement that has no basis in research

2 'First Impressions', Janine Willis and Alexander Todorov, *Psychological Science*, 1 July 2006

3 *Thinking, Fast and Slow,* Daniel Kahneman, May 2012

4 *Impressions Based on a Portrait Predict, 1-Month Later, Impressions Following a Live Interaction*, Gul Gunaydin, Emre Selcuk and Vivian Zayas, August 2016

5 'Women in the Workplace', McKinsey & Co, 30 September 2020

6 *Women & Power, A Manifesto*, Professor Mary Beard, 2 November 2017

7 Song first recorded in 1939 by Ella Fitzgerald and covered in 1982 by Fun Boy Three and Bananarama

8 BBC Radio 4 *Desert Island Discs*, 22 March 2020, https://www.bbc.co.uk/programmes/m000gm8m

9 *National Conversations,* Lauren Laverne talks to John Harris, 3 November 2011

10 'How to Dress for your Google Interview', Jason Warner, then head of staffing for a division of Google, *WIRED* magazine, 21 March 2007

11 'Life at the bar: Using your dress sense', Rachel Tandy, *The Lawyer*, 20 November 2014

12 Surgeon Captain Kate Prior speaking at a Diversity Project seminar on 21 April 2021

13 Research: Women Score Higher Than Men in Most Leadership Skills, Jack Zenger and Joseph Folkman, 25 June 2019, www.hbr.org

14 'Why We Should Be More Sexist', Tomas Chamorro-Premuzic TEDxCambridge, 13 June 2019

15 Body Image Survey, May 2019, www.mentalhealth.org.uk

16 11 Facts About Body Image, www.dosomething.org

17 '80 per cent of women are wearing the wrong bra size', by Jessica Davis, 'Harpers Bazaar', 11 September 2018, in discussion with Edita Solak, bra fitter at Victoria's Secret

18 Annie can be contacted via Instagram @justanniecastano

19 Castanohel scarves available at www.castanohel.com

20 Lyst 2020 Conscious Report

21 e.g. Patsy Rodenburg, The Second Circle, 9 October 2008, available on YouTube

22 *Strengthsfinder 2.0* from Gallup and Tom Rath

23 'Cosmetics as a Feature of the Extended Human Phenotype: Modulation of the Perception of Biologically Important Facial Signals', Nancy L. Etcoff, Shannon Stock, Lauren E. Haley, Sarah A. Vickery and David M. House, October 2011

24 'Consensus in Personality Judgements at Zero Acquaintance', Linda Albright, David A. Kenny and Thomas Malloy, October 1988

25 'Explaining financial and prosocial biases in favour of attractive people: Interdisciplinary perspectives from economics, social psychology, and evolutionary psychology', Dario Maestripieri et al, *Behav Brain Sci.*, January 2017

26 'Gender and the returns to attractiveness', Jaclyn S. Wong and Andrew M. Penner, *Research in Social Stratification and Mobility*, June 2016

27 *Dress Codes and Sex Discrimination – What You Need to Know*, Government Equalities Office, May 2018

28 Based on a survey of 3,500 British families with two opposite-gender parents conducted between 29 April and 15 May 2020, designed by researchers from the Institute of Fiscal Studies (IFS) and the UCL Institute of Education

29 Data also taken from the IFS and UCL survey

30 'Seven charts that show COVID-19's impact on women's employment', 8 March 2021 and 'Diverse employees are struggling the most during COVID-19 – here's how companies can respond', 17 November 2020 McKinsey & Co

31 'Flexible working: lessons from the pandemic', CIPD, 1 April 2021

32 *2020 Hiring Statistics, Trends & Data*, 19 February 2020, www.jobbatical.com

33 According to a Gartner, Inc. poll of 334 HR leaders conducted 13 April 2020

34 *Hamlet was Wrong*, Revisionist History podcast by Malcolm Gladwell, 6 August 2020

35 *How to ace a job interview with a robot recruiter*, cnbc.com 13 April 2021

36 *Why Meetings Go Wrong (And How to Fix Them)*, HBR IdeaCast Episode 708, *Harvard Business Review*

37 https://30percentclub.org/wp-content/uploads/2015/04/ Cracking-the-code.pdf

38 'Obesity discrimination in employment recruitment: "You're not hired!"' Stuart Flint et al, 2016 *Frontiers in Psychology*, Issue 7, p. 647

39 *Stella* magazine (*Sunday Telegraph*), 21 March 2021

40 *Sunday Telegraph*, Fashion, Spring/Summer 2021

41 *Unilever says no to 'normal' with new positive beauty vision* www. unilever.com, 9 March 2021

42 *Telegraph*, 20 March 2021

43 https://www.mentalhealth.org.uk/publications/how-to-mental-health

44 *Pregnancy and maternity discrimination forces thousands of new mothers out of their jobs*, Equality and Human Rights Commission, 24 July 2015

45 *Pregnancy and maternity discrimination research findings*, Equality and Human Rights Commission, 25 May 2018

46 'The Non-Issue', British *Vogue*, 2019

Index

Note: page numbers in **bold** refer to illustrations, page numbers in *italics* refer to information contained in tables.

Acknowledgements

First and foremost, a huge thank-you to my daughter Clara, beautiful in every way, who drew the illustrations for *Style and Substance,* alongside her many other commitments, and worked on the drawings until everyone was happy with their likeness.

Thank you to my dear husband Richard for all his encouragement and wise counsel – and his patience in reading several early drafts of a book clearly aimed at a different audience! My son Fitzroy, his wife Dyedra and my daughter Millie all also offered their input, advice and editing skills as the book took shape – thank you. I'm grateful to my family for bearing with me (mostly) patiently, as I've sought views and discussed ideas – and occasionally needed help with technology!

I am grateful to the friends, colleagues and inspiring women in business who so generously shared their thoughts and were happy for their fascinating stories to be told: Sarah Elliott, Birgit Neu, Beth Salmen, Suman Sidhu, Anne O'Leary, Kristy McKenzie, Asahi Pompey, Jenny Halpern Prince, Lucy Neville-Rolfe, Upasna Bhadhal, and to those I originally interviewed for an Instagram 'Friday Feature' – Janine Menasakanian, CJ Fildes and Sundiatu Dixon-Fyle. Thank you also to Annie Castano for so willingly sharing her expertise on colour. Thank you too to those who offered their thoughts under condition of anonymity – you know who you are!

A big thank-you to Stella McCartney for offering her insights around the important topic of sustainability and rethinking fashion.

And thank you to so many women I admire; friends who inspire through their style, their achievements and, most importantly, their generosity in helping other women succeed – you are proof that the ideas covered in this book are gathering momentum; that women are succeeding in our own way, bringing everything we offer to business, politics and creative fields: Mary Goudie, Anya Hindmarch, Nimco Ali, Melanie Richards, Niamh Corbett, Pavita Cooper, Jayne-Anne Gadhia, Liz Dimmock, Annaliese Jenkins and Anne Richards, to name but a few. And, of course, a big thank-you to those designers who are creating clothes that women want to wear to work today, for a variety of budgets, including Edeline Lee, Roksanda, Misha Nonoo, Samantha Cameron, Lisa Redman and Joanna Dai.

And, finally, a huge thank-you to Kruger Cowne for spotting the book's potential from a few rough ideas, and to Zoe Bohm and her colleagues at Little, Brown Book Group, who have been brimming with enthusiasm and expertise at every stage.